How to Sell Anything to Anybody

By the World's Greatest Salesman

JOE GIRARD

WITH STANLEY H. BROWN

SIMON AND SCHUSTER
NEW YORK

Designed by Elizabeth Woll
Manufactured in the United States of America

1   2   3   4   5   6   7   8   9   10

Library of Congress Cataloging in Publication Data
Girard, Joe.
How to sell anything to anybody.
Includes index.
1. Girard, Joe. 2. Sales personnel—
Biography. 3. Selling. I. Brown, Stanley H.,
joint author. II. Title.
HF5439.5.G57A33   658.85   77–21683
ISBN 0–671–22651–7

To my sainted mother in Heaven
for the love that saved my life
and helped me believe
that I was a worthwhile human being

Contents

8   CONTENTS

1

Introduction

You've got this book in your hands because you think it can help you get more out of your work—more money and more personal satisfaction. This probably isn't the first book about selling that you have read. Chances are you have seen and read a lot of other books, books that promise to give you the "secrets," the magic, the inspiration. You probably already know a lot about how to hype yourself by looking in the mirror every morning and repeating certain phrases to yourself. By now you know the mysteries of "PMLA" and "HPD" and some other magical-power expressions and attitude builders. You know a lot about what you should think and what you shouldn't think, positive and negative. And maybe you are a little confused by this time from all the contradictory advice the books have offered.

I don't want to take anything away from the promoters, the experts, and the other well-meaning people who grind out all those books. They have to make a living too.

But let's face it. What you want to know is how to sell real products and services now. And most of those authors never sold very much in their lives, except their books. They may be professional writers or professional sales training experts. Some of them may have spent a few weeks or months selling something until they figured out something at which they were better. And maybe one of them made a good living selling one multimillion-dollar real estate development every two years, which has nothing to do with the kind of selling you do and want to do better.

That's the point. They just aren't our kind of salesman, out there selling every day for a living. They don't do it because they have to. When you read their books, they sound fine. And they probably give you a little help, maybe even enough to earn back what they cost you. But when you think about those books, you realize pretty soon that these writers—even the best of them—just aren't our kind of salesman.

But I am. I sell cars and trucks. New ones, at retail, no fleet deals, just new cars and trucks, one at a time, face to face, belly to belly, to the same kind of people you sell, every day. Maybe you sell cars or suits or houses or appliances or furniture or something else, day in and day out, something that you have to sell a lot of to make out. And when you read these books by the experts, you probably have the same gut reaction I do: There's something missing. What is missing, your intuition tells you, is first-hand, on-the-job involvement with *our* problems, *our* people, *our* world. Those guys just don't feel like they've been out there in the trenches every day the way we have to be if we're going to eat tomorrow.

That's why my book is different. That's why this book is going to work for you in ways that the others never did. Because I'm out there every day the way you are. I do what you do. I feel what you feel. I want what you want. And I get it. Other people have been called the world's greatest salesman. But they aren't our kind of salesman. Among our kind of salesman,

I am the world's greatest. You don't have to take my word for that claim. If you want to check me out, take a look at the world's foremost authority, the *Guinness Book of World Records*. Look up the world's greatest salesman. You'll find that it's me, Joe Girard. Or check stories about me in *Newsweek*, *Penthouse*, and *Woman's Day*, or in a half-dozen other magazines and newspapers. You've probably seen me on one or another national television show in recent years. And they always introduce me as "the world's greatest salesman." These people don't make up stuff like that. They know before they talk. But if you still want to see for yourself, check the 1977 edition of the *Guinness Book of World Records*. It's all there, on page 345, or look in the business section if you don't have the 1977 issue. And I've been in there for four straight years.

How well have I done since I started selling in 1963? In my first year, I sold only 267 cars. Only! Even those days that would be more than just a living. In that first year, I was maybe the top guy in the dealership. In 1966, my fourth year, I sold 614 cars and trucks (retail). This is the year I became NUMBER ONE RETAIL CAR AND TRUCK SALESMAN IN THE WORLD. And every year since, I have been the NUMBER ONE RETAIL CAR AND TRUCK SALESMAN, increasing my business better than 10 percent a year and some years as high as 20 percent, even when we had bad recessions, layoffs, and long strikes. In fact, the worse the economy gets, the harder I work and the better I do. I have stayed on top even when the auto dealers in the Detroit area cut the workweek from six days to five.

Last year, 1976, was my biggest year. I had gross *earnings from commissions in excess of $200,000.* Not too many beat me, except maybe those guys who spend three years paying off some cabinet minister in some country to buy their airplanes or missiles. But that's not the kind of selling you and I are talking about.

What we are talking about is a profession that uses skills

and tools and experience and practice. It brings us lots of headaches and frustrations, no matter how well we do. But when we do it right, it brings us more financial and emotional pleasure than any other kind of work in the world. I do what I do because I love the money and the excitement and the satisfaction of winning again and again and again.

You may already be doing pretty well. You may have a home, a vacation place, a boat, and a couple of cars. But if you have read this far, you think there is more to be had than that. And you're right. There is more of all the kinds of pride and satisfaction every good salesman should feel. In fact, the better you are, the more you should want. If you think you have enough of everything, then you aren't doing as well as you could, so keep on reading. Because I have a total system for selling that is a lot like farming in a country where things grow all the time. With my system, you do a lot of things that are like planting seeds. You do them all the time, and then you begin to harvest—all the time. And every time you have harvested a sale, you plant something else. You plant and plant and harvest and harvest—all the time—through every season. There is nothing like it. I guarantee it.

But if you think that there is nothing you can do to sell and win, because you're a loser, let me tell you that I was a bigger loser than you have ever been.

For the first 35 years of my life I was the world's biggest loser. I got thrown out of high school. I got thrown out of about 40 different jobs. I lasted only 97 days in the U.S. Army. I couldn't even make it as a crook. I tried twice. The first time I wound up with nothing but a night of terror in juvenile detention. The second time the charges against me were dismissed for lack of evidence. And when I finally got into a business where I was making a small but fairly steady income, the first time I tried to expand I wound up facing bankruptcy, owing more money than I had ever seen, because I believed somebody who had no reason to tell me the truth.

How I got from there to here is what this book is about. Even now, I sell every day. This book is not being written by a spectator with a fancy title and a lot of degrees. This is being written by a working salesman who is in the front lines every day selling. Even when I travel around the country giving talks to other salesmen, I am selling, because salesmen have to be sold that the people who show them how to do it know how to do it because they do it. The story of how I got to be the world's greatest salesman gives me an enormous amount of pride. But I get even more from the letters I receive from working salesmen who meet me and hear me talk and then write telling me how I have changed their lives by making them better, happier, more prosperous salesmen.

Winning Bloodless Victories

Remember that for a real salesman there is nothing better than selling. It is like home runs for a hitter, touchdowns for a running back, victories for a general. But when a salesman sells there are no losers. Both the buyer and the seller win if it's a good sale. The confrontation that leads to a sale is like a game or a war, but one where nobody bleeds, nobody loses, everybody wins. What's better than that?

But the process that leads to that victory should start long before you ever see your prospect for the first time. And it goes on long after the customer signs the order, pays, and leaves with his purchase. In fact, if you think the sale ends when, like they say in the car business, you see the customer's taillights, you're going to lose more sales than you ever dreamed of. But if you understand how selling can be a continuing process that never ends, then you're going to make it to the big time.

Once my selling system got into high gear, I never had to look for customers among the people who walk into the front door of the showroom. I don't take "ups." All my customers these days are people who ask for me by name. All of them. And for every 10 sales I make, roughly 6 of them are to people I sold at least once before. And we're talking about automobiles. People buy them about every three or four years, and even less often among the middle- and working-class people who are most of my sales. If you're selling clothes or booze or things that people buy a lot more often, getting them back again and again is even more important. But it is harder to do with cars. So if I can show you the ways I keep people coming back to buy cars from me, you know it's going to mean even more sales for you if you're selling these other kinds of products and services where success depends even more on bringing them back again.

I guarantee you that my system will work for you, if you understand it and follow it. I look at selling situations and customers in different ways than I used to. This means that I have changed my attitudes about a lot of aspects of my profession. I know there are a lot of people who talk about the importance of attitudes. They tell you that if you change your attitude toward something they have put CAPITAL LETTERS on, then everything will be just dandy for you. Most of these people are sincere but they aren't out there selling face-to-face day after day.

Let's face it. We live in the real world, and it is a very tough world. Whatever you are selling, there is probably somebody else out there selling one exactly like it. Not probably. It's a fact. It is a very competitive world. And, aside from the thousands of Chevvy salesmen who are trying to sell exactly the same car to exactly the same customers as I am, there are hundreds of thousands of other salespeople trying to take the same money from them for everything from furniture, houses, swimming pools, and motorboats to vacation trips, tuition, and savings accounts. And when you finally get the customer to come in, he is looking to hustle you in some way, not because he is a bad person but because he has come to believe that you are. It is a very tough profession we have chosen, but if we choose to deal with it as a profession with rules and standards and principles, it can be made to pay off in financial and emotional satisfaction.

The first thing you'd better know—if you don't know it already—is that this is not always a nice world. Competition is a tough game, but everybody competes with everybody else for everything you and they want. I am no philosopher, but I knew that almost from the day I was born. And it is one of the few things I learned before the age of 35 that turned out to be useful to me. What I am trying to say is that the so-called experts are putting ideas in your way that you will either have to get rid of or reshape before they can help you make more money and have more satisfaction from selling.

It is a very tough, competitive world. But when I say that, I don't mean that you are going to have to cheat or steal to survive. Stick with me and you will see what I do mean. You will see how you can change people by selling them the right way, my way, and wind up with their money and their friendship. In fact, if you don't get both their money and their friendship, you are not going to be in business very long. Don't get me wrong: When I talk about friendship, I am not talking about goody-goody things like Love Thy Neighbor. How you get along with your neighbor is strictly your business. But when you get to the chapter on the Law of 250 you will understand exactly what I mean by friendship. We are going to deal with the kinds of attitudes customers have toward salesmen and the importance of telling the truth and the value of certain kinds of lies. If you don't understand whom you're dealing with and what they really want to hear, then you can't make it in the long run. I assure you of that.

But even before we get to the business of your customers' attitudes, we are going to have to deal with your own. Remember that I was a total loser for 35 years, which I am going to describe with enough detail so you'll start to feel sorry for me, like I felt sorry for myself. But I'll tell you right now that feeling sorry for yourself is a trap. It guarantees that you'll keep on losing. It kills everything that it takes to be a winner in the war of life and of selling. I'll show you that too. And I'll show you how I went from being a loser to being a big winner, the world's greatest salesman, like it says in the book. I did it all by myself. I'll tell you and show you how I did it. And you'll be able to see what you are doing in your own life that is defeating you and that can be turned around to make you a big winner.

I mean that. You'll have to do it to yourself and for yourself. Nobody can do it for you. But I believe that I can show you what I did with my life—and why I did it—so that you can be guided by it to look at yourself and your life and learn to turn the disadvantages into advantages, the liabilities into assets, the failures into successes, the defeats into victories.

Once you have come to that point, you get a set of attitudes built into your head. I know that most of those so-called experts tell you to do it the other way around. That is, they give you the words, the attitudes that you ought to have, and they tell you to develop them. They tell you to make yourself believe them by repeating them every morning when you get up or by saying them to yourself in the mirror or some such thing as that.

The Way to Winning Attitudes

But if you do that without knowing why or how, it's not going to be worth any more than squeezing a rabbit's foot or rubbing a lucky piece. The only way to have the right attitudes is to know what the wrong ones are and how you got them and why you keep them. And I am going to lead you through the story of my attitudes: the wrong ones, and then the great change in my life that led me to the right ones. Don't get the idea that I'm referring to some magical moment when a finger from heaven touched me. The change in my life came for a lot different and more understandable reasons, as you will discover.

I am not saying that what I went through was easy, but I did it. And if I could do it, coming from where I came from, anybody who is sick and tired of being a loser can do it. I guarantee that too. But you have to build in your own version of the right attitudes as the first step. Then you will understand the other rules and parts of my system, and why they work if you work them properly and consistently. The Law of 250 will make it clear why you will want to use the system all the time. When we get to the use of time, you will understand not just the obvious facts about the value of time and the cost of wasting it, but also the importance of being realistic about yourself and what you can do, and how to be good to yourself in the long and the short run. When we get to certain aspects of what I do, I will of course be talking about how I sell cars to people. I will relate what I do to what salespeople in other fields do. A lot of it is obvious and you can figure it out for yourself. When I say it is essential to get a customer to take a demonstration ride, you know, if you're selling houses, that the equivalent is getting the people into the model. Or putting the suit on the customer. Or even cooking them a meal if you're selling them a new kitchen. The old-time door-to-door vacuum cleaner salesman used to throw dust and dirt on the floor and then run the vacuum to show how well it worked. The Club Aluminum salesman cooks a meal when he shows his line. A mattress salesman has got to get the customer to lie down. Those obviously are all equivalents of the demonstration ride in a new Chevrolet.

But whatever I do and say that has to do with selling cars, there is almost always an equivalent for selling anything else. Maybe a life insurance salesman can't get you to go to your own funeral like Tom Sawyer did, but he'll get you to talk about your wife and children, and maybe get you to take out their pictures and leave them on the table while he is talking. This can be a helluva good reminder that you're not going to be around forever, and this may be all he needs to remind you of. It's a kind of demonstration ride.

From here on out, I am going to take you step by step through my discovery of the way to change from loser to winner. I'll show you how I built in the attitudes of a sure winner and how those attitudes led me to the development of my system. And remember this: Those attitudes and that system have made me the World's Greatest Salesman.

2

The End of a Loser, the Beginning of a Winner

Somebody once told me that I was a born salesman. Let me tell you that's not true. Some salesmen, maybe even most salesmen, may be born to it. But I was not born a salesman. I made me a salesman, all by myself. And if I could do it, starting from where I did, anybody can. Stay with this story and you'll soon see what I mean.

Lots of people start out poor, but the way it was where I was born was a special kind of poor, maybe something like the kind of poor these days if you're black and poor. I was born November 1, 1928, on the lower east side of Detroit. In those days it was almost all what you would call Italian, but what I call Sicilian, because to me there's a big difference. I'm proud to be a Sicilian, even though a lot of people, including people from other parts of Italy, discriminate against us and try to make out that all of us are born into some kind of crime syndicate. My strong pride got me into a lot of trouble in my younger days, and even sometimes in recent years. I was pretty quick to fight anybody who called me "wop," "dago," or "greaser." I know that everybody is prejudiced against somebody, but I have never liked it directed against me, and I've bloodied a lot of noses for being called "wop," "dago," or "greaser."

The first home I remember was an upper flat in a two-family house across the street from a coal yard. You would think it was a pretty lousy place if you lived across from a coal yard. But it had one advantage. When things were really tough in the wintertime, and the house was freezing cold, my older brother Jim and I could go across the street and I would crawl under the fence and throw hunks of coal to my brother, who would put them in a burlap bag. Then we'd haul them home and put them in the furnace. Sometimes that was all there was to burn, so it never bothered us that the coal maybe belonged to somebody else. That's the kind of world I was born into.

The furnace was in the cellar, but I remember the cellar for another reason. It was my father's favorite place to beat me from as early as I can remember. I guess I was as good and bad as most little kids, nothing special. So I never knew why he did it to me and not to my brother or my two younger sisters. But he did it. Mostly he would take me down there and tie me to a pipe, and then he'd beat me with one of those big leather straps he used to sharpen his razor. Any time any of the kids made any noise or anything, it was me that got it. Down to the cellar, and him hollering as he whipped me, *You're no good, you'll never be nothing, you're gonna go to jail*—stuff like that. And I never could figure out why me, but he never stopped as long as I lived at home.

Sometimes I'd run away a few blocks to the railroad yard down by the river and hide out in the boxcars. Once in a while, I'd even sleep on the straw-covered floors of freight cars. And when I'd come home, he'd beat me again and tell me I was no good and would never amount to anything, and that I'd end up in Jacktown (what we called the state prison

in Jackson, Michigan, where a lot of guys from the neighborhood went).

I'll tell you one thing. If you grow up in a house where
your father is the boss, and he tells you you're no damn good
from the earliest time you can remember and beats you hard
while he's telling you, you believe it. After all, he's the only
father, the only authority you know, and he must be right.
After a while, I started believing it, even though my mother
used to come down to the cellar afterward and tell me that I
really was a good boy. That helped some, I guess, but she was
not the boss like my old man, so, as much as I loved her, I still
believed that I was no good and never would be worth anything. I believed it for a long time, and it had a lot to do with
what happened to me, what I did to myself, for most of my
life.

I have tried to figure out what it was that made him hate
me and pick on me and dump on me that way all the time. He
came from Sicily as a young man, uneducated, practically illit-
erate, and poor. His own father had been a tyrant who cursed
and beat him. My father was 25 when he married my mother.
She was only 15, and her mother was not too happy about
her marrying my father. Nobody ever told me what was going
on in those days, but a feud started between my father and
my mother's mother that never ended as long as he lived. My
father wouldn't let any of us, including my mother, have anything to do with my grandmother, even when she lived in the
same two-family house. My mother used to sneak into the
cellar and talk to her through a partition sometimes. And I
would visit her too, because we were very close friends, maybe
because of how my father felt about us. Whenever my father
found out that I was seeing his enemy, bam, the beating and
the hollering and the cursing began again.

You're probably wondering what this has to do with how to
sell. Well, it has everything to do with how attitudes get
planted in your head. And what got planted in my head was

that I was no good and that I wouldn't amount to anything. I believed that, and I was going to prove that my father was right. After all, you're supposed to honor and obey your father. But there was another attitude planted there too, from the same beatings and cursings. There was this feeling of wild anger against him and wanting to prove to him that he was wrong, so he'd love me like he loved my brother and my sisters. Sometimes one attitude operated, sometimes the other one, and sometimes they canceled each other out.

My father was never able to get much work. After all, it was the Depression and we were Sicilians in Detroit and he had no trade, nothing. Mostly he was laid off or on the WPA. We were almost always on welfare (which they called relief in those days), and about the only happy times I can remember were around Christmas when the Goodfellows (a local charity) would send us this box of toys that people had contributed. Mostly they were used and repaired, but it was a big thrill. And even better was the coupon they gave that we could take downtown and exchange for a pair of new shoes. That was a very big deal to me in those days.

When I was around eight years old, I started working. A few blocks from where we lived there were a lot of factories. U.S. Rubber had a tire plant near the river, there was a big stove factory, and there were some furniture factories and some others. All along East Jefferson Avenue, near these plants, there were workingmen's bars. I built a shoeshine box and got some brushes and polishes (I don't remember where I got the money for them), and I worked those bars giving shines. If you think you have earned money the hard way, let me tell you that squatting on the floors of crummy saloons shining shoes for pennies will match whatever you've done. I'd start out in the afternoon after school when the factories were letting out. I'd work all the bars along Jefferson for about a mile, and then I'd come back and start again, maybe more than once in a day. My price was a nickel, if I could get it. Sometimes I'd get a tip of an extra penny or two, and sometimes I couldn't even get more than two cents for the whole shine. After a while, I developed some tricky moves like tossing the brushes in the air and changing hands. People got to know me, and I'd get extra tips. In those days of the 1930s, even one penny bought a lot of candy, and a nickel bought a double-dip ice cream cone or a quart of milk.

The second and third time along the street I'd see the same guys three or four drinks later. I saw what booze does to people just in the course of a few hours. Sometimes it would make them easier and maybe more generous, but a lot of times it just made them meaner. After all, these were men who had worked a hard day and were maybe scared they'd lose their jobs. There were more workers than jobs in those days, a lot more. And they had stopped off to unwind and unload their troubles before they had to go home to a poor and miserable house. Working those bars was pretty grim. But I'd work till maybe ten or eleven at night and come home with about a dollar, sometimes more. All of it went to the family, and sometimes it was all the money that was coming in. When a plant was closed or there wasn't much business for me for some other reason and I only brought home a few cents, my father would holler at me and beat me. Those nights I'd be afraid to go home. The fear of not doing well got built into me then, and I'd want to stay out later to do maybe a few more shines.

It was a lousy kind of childhood, but I never want to forget it. That's why I keep a big picture of me at age nine on my knees shining a shoe. I have it hanging on the wall of my office so I won't forget what I started from. I hated it, but I'm proud of it.

My First Sales

Maybe there was a little selling experience in going around and practically begging guys to let me shine their shoes. I guess putting on my little act on the floor with the brushes and all was a kind of selling pitch. But where I really learned about one aspect of selling was when I started delivering newspapers. I'd get up at about six o'clock in the morning and go to the garage where the Detroit *Free Press* copies were dropped off to be delivered in the neighborhood. I'd fold them and carry them in a bag on my route, and then go to school and do the shine bit afterward.

Where I really learned about selling, though, was when the paper had a contest for new subscribers. For every one you signed up who stayed for at least a month, you won a case of Pepsi-Cola. Now that was a very big deal to me. A case of 24 12-ounce bottles of soda pop was really something. You talk about incentives and motivation. Boy, that really was it for me. I worked every house and every apartment on every street I could find. I rang so many doorbells my fingers got sore. I may even have missed a day or two of school during that contest. But I was persistent. I'd say, "We're having a contest, and I'd like you to sign up for just one week." The prize was only if they lasted a month, but I figured that most people would keep taking the paper once they had signed up. I'd tell them how it would be delivered to their door before they got up, which was true. And if they said no, I'd keep on going, never giving up, never being so disappointed that I didn't keep pushing doorbells. It's no fun being turned down. But I soon found out that the more people I talked to, the more sales I made. And that is fun, and better than fun. Because pretty soon the little garage we had behind our house was lined with cases of Pepsi that I could sell in the neighborhood for whatever I could get for them. This gave me more money to bring home, more hope that I could prove to my father that I was worth something. But even that didn't seem to work.

I stayed with the shine box and the newspapers for about five years, going to school most of the time but not doing very well at it. I was not much of a scholar, but I learned some and didn't do too bad when I was there. But the trouble between my father and me never got any better. And maybe a couple of dozen different times he would throw me out of the house. I'd sleep in those boxcars, or sometimes I'd go downtown and take a room in a flophouse at the edge of downtown. It was a crummy part of town, cheap hotels, roominghouses, whorehouses, movies that showed what passed for porn in those days. I'd get a bed in one of those places for a dime or a quarter a night—you didn't get a room, just a bed in a kind of dormitory with a bunch of drunks sleeping if off or having the dt's. My father would come looking for me after a while and bring me back home and tell me to be good. He did it because my mother made him do it, I guess. I'd come home, try school for a while, hang out with the guys on the corner, and then get thrown out again.

When I was 16, I was out on the corner one night with these two guys, two friends of mine from the neighborhood. They said, "We're going to knock off this bar over on Meldrum and Lafayette. We cased the joint already and there's liquor and maybe he leaves some cash. Wanna come along?" It was one of the bars where I used to shine shoes, and I knew the bar. I'd never done anything like that before, but maybe it was because I knew the place or whatever, but I decided to go along with them. Whatever I was, I wasn't a crook. At least not till then. I don't know what decided me to go along, but there I was.

When they cased the bar, one of the guys had gone to the john and left the window open. In those days you could do that. Now there would be bars on the windows and alarms and a meter to tell the night man that the window wasn't locked. But not then, even in a crummy, poor neighborhood like we lived in.

So about ten o'clock that night we sneaked into the garage of the Whittier Hotel, which used to be a classy apartment hotel down on the river. We copped a car, I remember it was a Studebaker. I can still hear the garage guy hollering, "Hey, come back with that car." But we just tore ass out of that place and stashed the car on a side street in the neighborhood.

Bars in Detroit close at two in the morning, so we had to wait till the night men closed the place, cleaned up, and left. It was around three-thirty in the morning when we hit the place. We got the car and drove into the alley behind the bar. There was nobody around on the streets or anywhere. The whole area was completely closed down for the night. I wasn't even very scared while it was going on. In fact, once we got there, I wasn't even scared at all.

One of the guys crawled through the window and unlocked the back door. Then we just loaded up the car with all the cases of liquor we could fit into it. It was in the days of World War II. It must have been sometime around May of 1944, and booze was still pretty hard to get. In fact, they rationed it for a while in Michigan. Anyway, once we got the car loaded and cleaned out the register, we took off and hid the booze and split up the money. There was $175 in the till, so my share was nearly $60 plus the buck a bottle we got from selling the liquor to other guys who hung out on the corner. For me that was big easy money, and the whole thing worked so well that I didn't think anything more about it.

It's funny when I think back to those days, because I really don't know why I didn't keep on doing it after that first job. I mean I wasn't that scared or anything, and the money was good, and it figured that we could find other jobs as easy to do. But I didn't do it. I think my old man was bugging me a lot to get a job, and I did get one in some factory. So maybe I was more afraid of him and what he'd do if I didn't go to work.

Anyway, I practically forgot about the whole thing, or at least I was trying to, when one day I'm lying in bed at home and I hear a lot of commotion. My mother was crying, and I couldn't figure out what was happening. It never occurred to me that it could have anything to do with breaking into the bar. That had happened three months before, and I hadn't had anything to do with those guys after that, and nobody had said anything about it again.

All of a sudden a guy is in my room and he is shoving me and saying, "Get up!" I open my eyes, and a badge is shoved in my face and this cop says, "Get your clothes on." The next thing I know I'm at the police station, and this cop and a bunch of others are asking me about the bar burglary and a bunch of jobs pulled at bars and grocery stores I didn't know anything about. But they knew about the one I had been in on. One of the guys had been caught and told about a bunch of jobs he'd done, including that bar, and somehow my name came up. So the next thing I'm in the juvenile detention home. It was the worst place I'd ever been, a big room full of cots and kids, and this big guy comes around with a strap and makes a kid bend over and starts whipping him. It was worse than a night I spent in a flophouse, where they turned on the lights in the middle of the night to haul out the body of a wino who had died during the night. It was the worst night I had ever spent in my life, and I had spent a lot of nights in a lot of horrible places.

In the morning they brought me out to see the man who owned the bar we robbed. He remembered me and asked me why I did it. I said I didn't know, but that I'd pay him back what I had taken. He said O.K. and didn't press charges, so I got out of that place. I would have done anything to get out of there.

My father and my uncle came to get me out. My father started beating me as soon as we got outside the building. He beat me in the car, and he beat me when we got home. He kept hollering about the shame I had brought to the family name. This time I really thought I had it coming to me. I had proved to my father that what he had always said about me was true—I was no good, a small-time crook, and I had got arrested.

But I also got the scare of my life, spending that night in

the juvenile home. No matter what happened, I wasn't going to go through that again. I wasn't going to go to jail like a lot of guys I hung out with wound up doing.

So I took a job at the stove company in the neighborhood where a lot of the Sicilians worked. I put insulation into the stove panels, which was a rotten job because the stuff got into your clothes and your skin and your nose and all. And they worked you hard and fast. One day I got caught smoking—it was my second offense—and they broomed me. Broom, that's a word we used for getting fired. It's like you're a piece of garbage and they sweep you out, which is how I felt about myself a lot of the time.

I keep thinking that I had about 40 different jobs in those days, but I can't really count them all. I drove a truck for a printer until I got broomed for taking too long on deliveries. I worked at Chrysler Motors making armrests for Imperials. That wasn't too bad. I worked at Hudson Motor Car on the assembly line, which is one of the worst jobs there is because you are attached to the machines and they decide how hard you work. I worked at an electroplating factory where the place was full of vats of hot acid and molten metal, with fumes that got into your lungs. I've had asthma ever since then.

I was a busboy at the Statler Hotel for a while. Another time I was a bellhop at the Book-Cadillac Hotel, which became the Sheraton. I did a little act there, wearing one of those uniforms and paging guests. One day I threw away a bunch of telegrams instead of delivering them to the rooms. I denied that it had happened while I was there, but they were time-stamped, and I didn't know that. So they broomed me. I sometimes think that if I had known things like that I might have done better, and maybe even got to be a vice president of something like the Sheraton. But I was pretty ignorant in those days.

I was in and out of school a lot, and somewhere along the line I got in a fight with the study hall counselor at Eastern

High School, and I got expelled. He kept picking on me, maybe for nothing, maybe just for the sort of things that kids do, but then he started at me talking about "you people" and how "you people had better learn" and all that. I told him that my name wasn't "you people," because you know what it means when they start saying "you people." He was talking about Italians, and pretty soon it got kind of nasty and I hit him, and that was all for me and school.

As I remember it, I lost most of my jobs for getting in fights with guys who talked about "wops" and "dagos" and "guineas." Maybe I was just looking for trouble in those days. Maybe I just wanted to keep losing to show my father that he was right and that I was no good. But I was full of anger, and there were a lot of bigots around in those days to take it out on.

That night in the juvenile detention home may have saved me from worse. I'll never forget how I felt. Maybe I was no good, but I sure as hell wasn't bad enough to deserve that.

After some more drifting from one lousy job to the next, I enlisted in the army. That was at the beginning of 1947. But I fell off a truck and hurt my back during basic training, and they gave me a discharge. But even that didn't come easy. I hated the army. It was almost as bad for me as being in jail. But for a while they just gave me barracks duty instead of letting me out. Then one day a sergeant I'd never seen offered to help me get a discharge if I would give him my mustering-out pay. For a while I thought it was some kind of a setup, and that they were trying to catch me bribing an officer. He kept at me and I tried to ignore him. When my case finally came up and they gave me the discharge, he came and asked for his money. I gave it to him and went home with an honorable discharge. I don't know if he had anything to do with it or not, but I was so glad to get out of there that I gave him the few bucks that I had been paid. When I got home, my mother was glad to see me, but my father started in again with what a bum I was. He told me that not even the army wanted me. He said, "You are no good and you'll never be any good." He said that he should have choked me when I was born. I'll never forget that day as long as I live. With tears in my eyes, hearing my father screaming and hollering all over again, and seeing the tears in my mother's eyes, I left home, working sometimes and hanging out other times, still hearing the screaming and the hollering of my dad's voice, which constantly haunted me.

Then, in 1948, I got into some more trouble with the law for being stupid. Another guy and I opened a hat cleaning and blocking and shoeshine shop in our neighborhood. In the back room we had blackjack and dice games. We thought we had worked out a pretty good system of watching out for the law. One of us would be a lookout in the front of the store, and if somebody who looked like a cop came in, we had a signal with a nail through the wall. The guy in back was supposed to swallow the dice or run away so there would be no evidence. One day I was up front, and an old buddy from my days at Barbour Junior High School came in. We talked about the old days and he said he was in the construction business. Then he asked to go into the back and I let him in. When my partner saw him, he recognized that he was a cop and ran out the back way with the dice.

The Hard Way to Easy Money

It never entered my mind that somebody from our neighborhood could be a cop. It was kind of an insult to even suggest that somebody was a cop. In fact, there's a Sicilian curse that tells a guy he should be a cop. But this guy was a cop. Even though my partner got away with the gambling evidence so that all we had was a friendly card game going on, they gave everybody tickets for loitering. The rule with our kind of joint was that the guys who ran it had to pay the fines when the customers got hit for loitering. So our little business ended up with us holding a stack of tickets we had to pay the fines on. That was the end of my days as a gambling house operator.

And it was just as well, because until we got raided, we were making pretty easy money. And for a while I really believed there was such a thing as easy money, even though I had worked my ass off for most of the money I ever earned in my life.

Then there was another string of lousy jobs, fighting, getting broomed, and hanging around with the guys, shooting snooker or whatever else I could do. Sometimes I think that if anybody in those days had treated me decently, I might have stayed on a job and worked my way up to something good. But maybe the reason nobody treated me decently was that I really believed I was no good and acted bad to prove it. I really think I was acting rotten so that my father would know he was right, and then maybe he would love me. I know that sounds crazy, but that's the way people seem to act a lot of the time. Look at the guys who try to make girls love them by beating them and even killing them. It makes no sense, but that seems to be the way people act when they are angry with the world for not treating them right.

I finally did get a break from one man, and that started to change my life a little. His name was Abe Saperstein, and he was a very small-scale home builder. What he did was buy up vacant lots in different neighborhoods and hire some people and build small cheap houses on the lots, one at a time, maybe a half dozen or so a year. He wasn't building any Levittown, just a nickel-and-dime operation. He hired me as a common laborer, which was all I could do. I drove a truck, mixed cement, hauled building materials, and worked at bricklaying and everything else on the houses. In those days, Saperstein built them for maybe $9,000 and sold them for maybe $12,000. There wasn't much selling, and what there was he did himself so he wouldn't have to pay commissions. It was mostly about getting money from the bank—mortgages and all that. People needed cheap houses, and they bought them if they could finance them.

It was such a small operation that I got to see how practically everything was done, and who was brought in to do what we couldn't do ourselves. I got married about the time I came to work for Saperstein, and then our first child was on the way. That and the fact that Saperstein treated me well and let me learn the business kept me there. It was probably the first job I ever had that I stayed on more than a year. It was no big deal, but it was a living, enough to feed my wife, my son Joe, and my daughter Grace.

When Saperstein decided to retire, he turned the business over to me. That was not really as big as it sounded because all we had was an old truck, some tools, and a little cement mixer. But I had learned how to put that and some experience together and run it on my own. Detroit's economy has a lot of ups and downs, even more than other places. But in a good year I could build enough houses, one at a time, scattered around town, to keep things going and make a little more money than I could make on an ordinary job.

Things went pretty well for a while. But it was strictly small time. If you got two vacant lots together, you could save money by having two foundations dug at the same time, buying enough materials and labor to do both together. Even that was larger scale than what we usually did. But it didn't take a genius to see the advantages of getting bigger. So I decided to expand the operation somehow.

Saperstein was a decent man. He treated me like a son, and I loved the guy. He taught me a lot, as I moved from truck driver to supervisor to owner. But what I didn't learn was whom to trust and whom not to trust. With the kind of small business we had, trust wasn't important. Nobody trusted us for much for long.

So when I went on my own, I didn't know that you're not supposed to believe anything unless you see it in writing. I started looking around for a piece of land where I could build a bunch of houses at one time. All the subcontracting and all the materials could be bought and delivered cheaper. Finally I found a parcel of land in the suburbs northeast of Detroit. I could build about 50 houses all in one place, and I could build at least four at a time and put them up a lot cheaper that way than the way I was doing it.

The reason the land was available at a price I could afford was that it was completely undeveloped—mainly meaning no sewers. And around Detroit people wouldn't buy houses with septic tanks. At first I wasn't interested in the tract. But then the salesman said, "Don't worry about sewers. I was at City Hall in Mount Clemens and I heard the word that they were going to start building the sewers out here in the spring. But don't tell anybody I told you, because they don't want to start a lot of land speculation around here."

Great! That's what I wanted to hear, so I bought the property on a land contract at a very high rate of interest. But that was O.K., because once I got a model home built and started selling from it, there would be a lot of money coming in. It looked like a sure thing.

I built the first house, put up signs and ran ads, and waited. To keep operating costs down, I was going to do the selling myself. Every weekend, I'd go out there and sit in that house. Weekends are when people have the time to shop for homes. A lot of people came around to look, and they liked what they saw. The price was right and there was a lot of buyer interest.

But they all asked the same question: Are there sewers? I told them what I knew, that the sewers would be in in a few months. So they said they would come back when the sewers were in. And I sat there and waited. Meanwhile, I owed money on the land and on the building materials. There is a lot of short-term credit in the building business. You get your money out when you start selling. But I wasn't selling anything, and the short-term credit was getting to be long-term. Everybody was dunning me for money. I was in the hole for about $60,000.

It finally dawned on me that I had better find out damned

quick about those sewers. So I went to City Hall out there and asked, and everybody looked at me funny: What sewers? There were no plans for sewers then or ever, I soon found out. In fact, they haven't built sewers out there yet. I never felt so stupid in my life, believing that real estate salesman on a thing like that without checking. But I did believe him, and everything I had done—staying out of trouble, working hard—for ten years was down the drain.

Finally it got to the point where, when I came home at night, I would have to park the car a couple of blocks away and sneak into my own house through the alley and over the back fence. The bank was trying to repossess my car.

Nowhere to Go but Up

Then one night I came home and June, my wife, asked me for money for groceries. I didn't have any. "What are the kids going to eat?" she asked.

How about that for a question: What are the kids going to eat? Here I was a home builder who allowed himself to be conned to the point where everything was gone. Creditors were on my tail. The bank was after my house and car. Bad enough, but now nothing to eat. I sat up the whole night wondering what to do. For a while the old feelings kept coming back. I was no good, like my father always said. No matter how hard I tried to straighten out my life, it came back to that. But I couldn't forget that question my wife had asked. There was no time to feel sorry for myself. I had responsibilities to other people, to my wife and children, besides the money I owed to my subcontractors and suppliers for work that they had done in good faith. But I wasn't worried at that moment about debts or bankruptcy or my car. Pretty soon all I could think about was getting enough money to feed my family the next day. That was all. Just keeping them from being hungry another day. I had known a lot of hunger when

I was a kid, when all we ate at home every day was spaghetti, lots of times without even any sauce or anything on it. I was the biggest loser ever. But I was not going to make other people suffer because of what I did or didn't do. I had always made a living for my family. As a kid, I was sometimes the only support. When I worked in factories and made $90 a week, my father made me hand over the checks and gave me a couple of bucks for spending money. I always had been able to bring home enough to feed my wife and children—maybe not fancy, but enough—until that moment.

I didn't spend too much time thinking about how dumb I had been to believe that real estate salesman. If I had, I might have realized that believing him without checking was maybe another way of ruining myself to prove to my father that he was right and that I was no good. Though by then I had helped him finance and build a little house he lived in during his last years. All I thought about was finding some honest way to get food for my family.

That was how I got into the car-selling business. That was the start of my becoming the world's greatest salesman.

Look back to learn how to look forward better.

3

It All Begins
with Want

The idea of selling cars for a living had occurred to me before
that day. In fact, I had a friend who was a car salesman, and
when my building business started going sour, I asked him a
few times to get me a job as a salesman. But he never took
me seriously and kept brushing me off, telling me that I didn't
know anything about selling.

In a way that was true. My experience selling houses didn't
count for much, because, at the low prices I was charging for
the few I built, there was no selling. People were glad to get
them. All I had to do was sit in the model, make the deal, and
arrange for the paper work. I probably learned more about
selling when I shined shoes and sold produce in the streets
from the back of a truck than I ever learned selling houses.
With the drunks in the bars and the housewives on the street,
getting them to notice you and like you was important if you
wanted to make a little extra or even to make the sale in the
first place. I always had some sense of that. I always had
some idea that the way I got a guy to take a shine or to give

me an extra tip, or the way I got a housewife to take a dozen ears of corn instead of six was to sell *me* to them.

But at this point in my life, all I could think of was getting some kind of work right away. My friend in the car business brushed me off again, so I went to see another man I knew in the business. He was sales manager of a Chevrolet dealership. Right away he explained why I had been getting the brushoff. Car salesmen, he said, always feel that there are only a certain number of customers and too many other salesmen. They feel that every time a new salesman comes into the showroom, he is going to take sales away from them.

I had suffered from another handicap since I was a kid and that was that I stuttered badly from the time I was about eight. It seemed to have started from my father beating me. For years it caused me a lot of painful embarrassment, but the kind of work I was able to get didn't require me to have to speak well. I had talked to a lot of people about it, including doctors. They all said pretty much the same thing: try to talk slower. I tried a lot and I guess it got better sometimes, but there just wasn't all that much pressure on me to improve my speech—until I started selling cars.

Then I had to do something. And what I had to do was teach myself to concentrate on what I was trying to say and to say it slowly and carefully. I was thirty-five when I really began working on it. And I soon learned to overcome that handicap, because I had to, otherwise we weren't going to eat.

Learning to overcome stuttering was one of the most important things that happened to me when I started selling. Because it made me think about what I was trying to say and what I should say and what people wanted to hear. That is something that everybody who sells should do all the time of course. But having that handicap forced me to do it. I not only cured myself of stuttering that way. I also learned some of the fundamentals of communication, because I learned to listen and to plan every word I said carefully. It wasn't long before I had got to the point where I almost never stuttered and I almost always said what I wanted to say exactly right.

I had bought cars and I knew that the way the business worked was that the salesmen stood in a group and when the door opened, whoever was next came up to the customer. But I was desperate, so I said to this fellow, "How about if I don't take any floor time from other salesmen?" He looked at me kind of funny, because it didn't make sense. "What if I just get customers in other ways than taking turns on the floor." So he said O.K. and I was hired. But that didn't mean anything, because salesmen in that place didn't get any "draw." In fact, they didn't even get a demonstrator to drive until they got to a certain selling level.

I had made my arrangement and I was a salesman, but I had no idea where I was going to find customers. I knew that people worked lists, but I didn't know what lists were and how you got them. The only list I knew about was the telephone book. So I figured I'd tear a couple of pages out of the directory. What the hell, it was a list, and everybody on it had a telephone number. In fact, I tore out two white pages, and then I figured that business people use trucks and most people aren't home during the day anyway, so I tore out two yellow pages.

That was my first prospect list—four pages from the Detroit telephone directory. It wasn't much, but it was better than nothing.

I am sure this would make a dandy story if I said that the first number I picked at random brought me a prospect who came in that day and bought a car from me. Maybe I would tell you that if I thought you would believe it.

The First Car Sale I Ever Made

No. I made my first sale that day, but it wasn't from a phone call. As a matter of fact, it was from a customer who walked into the showroom just before closing, when all the guys were either busy with customers or on their way home.

He walks in and there is no one else there. I look around for about a second, remembering that I had said I wouldn't take any other salesman's floor time. But I was keeping my promise, because nobody was there. And by that time I was so desperate that I would have fought anybody who got in my way.

Lots of guys frame the first dollar they took in at their new store. And they can recall every detail of the first sale they ever made in their business. You might think that I can recall every detail of that first sale. Or, if I can't, you might think it would be good for this book if I made up a story about that first sale. But I won't do that. I'll tell you frankly that I don't remember the man's name. I don't remember what kind of car he bought.

I remember two things about that first sale. Just two things. One was that he was a Coca-Cola salesman. I probably remember that because it had something to do with grocery stores, and groceries were on my mind a lot that day. The other thing I remember was the feeling I had from the first time I saw the guy that there was no way he was going to get out without buying a car from me. To this day I cannot remember his face, and for a very simple reason: Whenever I looked at him, all I saw was what I wanted from him. And my want was a bag of groceries to feed my family.

I don't remember the pitch I made. I didn't know much about cars or selling or anything in those days, so I know I didn't talk product to him. I had never heard the drill about answering objections, but I am sure that however he stalled, I got him moving again. If he pulled the one about the wife, I am sure that I handed him the phone or got up to drive over with him to his house. I don't know anything more about that man except that he represented the only way I had at that moment to straighten out my bent life and fulfill my obligations to my family. He was a bag of groceries, and if I sold him, they would eat.

Want. My want. That was all I knew. And that want was

enough to drive me to say and do enough of the right things to sell him a car. I am not saying that that's all there is to it, then or now. But that is most of it. If you want, and know what you want, you will have most of what you need to be a successful salesman. I mean that. Nobody can be a great salesman without wanting. Wanting something very much. And the more you want, the more you drive yourself to do what it takes to sell.

Maybe the reason that I'm the world's greatest salesman is that there really isn't anything much that you can want more than feeding your hungry family. That doesn't mean that you have to have a hungry family or somebody who needs an operation to save their life or something just as grim in order to sell cars or anything else. But you have to want something. And you have to know what it is. And you have to see every move you make as a way of getting whatever it is you want.

Once I saw that Coca-Cola salesman as a bag of groceries to bring home to my family, he was sold, whether he knew it or not. I can't think of anything I have ever wanted as much as that bag of groceries. But I have wanted a lot of other things. I always know what they are and I try to tie every phone call, every word I say to every customer into fulfilling that want.

First, you have to know what you want. Second, you have to know that you can get it if you sell the next prospect.

You may think that's a little too simple. You're right. But it's just slightly oversimplified. Because it made me a salesman that first day. I didn't know from nothing except my own want and the fact that if I sold this guy, I would get those groceries. And I did it. I sold him and then I talked the sales manager into lending me $10 to buy a bag of groceries for my family. Don't tell me it doesn't work.

Knowing what you want will power your drive.

4

The Mooch Is a Human Being

I don't know what term you use in your town and in your business to talk about a customer. But in Detroit, in the retail car business, he's The Mooch. It's a terrible expression, because it's a terrible way to think of somebody who is coming in to give you money. It creates a negative attitude toward this person who wants to buy something from you.

Now that I have said that, I want to point out that salesmen around here don't use that word for no reason at all, no matter how much it may harm their performance. There are reasons why salesmen feel hostile toward prospects, and even toward customers. I understand those reasons and so do you. But I try very hard not to think of a customer as The Mooch. Because words in your head can become destructive.

But let's take a look at the way we perceive customers, and at what they really are. First of all, they are people, human beings with the same kinds of feelings and needs that we have, even though we tend to think of them as a different breed.

Where I sell most of the people who come in to buy cars are working class, and they work hard for their money—very hard. And for most of them, whatever money they spend with us is money they won't have to spend on something else they want and need. I don't think any of this comes as news to you, but I am sure that, just like me, you forget it a lot of times.

That's because we are professionals whose time is worth money, and every day we see a lot of people who don't seem to be serious about anything but taking up our time. That's really the problem. That's really the reason we think of a person as The Mooch, or whatever term you use where you come from.

The thing to remember is that when a customer comes in, he's a little scared. (By the way, when I say "he" it is just for convenience. About 30 percent of my customers are women buying cars on their own, so what I really mean is "he or she.") That person is probably there to buy. I say "probably," because we know that there are a lot of shoppers in the world. But mostly, whether they are aware of it or not, they are interested in what you are selling. Interested enough to be converted into buyers, even when they are only shopping. But they're scared. They're scared of parting with $30 for a pair of shoes, $100 for a suit, or $5,000 for a car. That's money, and it comes hard. So they're scared. Scared of you too, because they all know or think they know that salesmen are out to get them.

That's not really true for most of us. But once they walk in the door, a lot of them start to panic a little. They're just looking. They want to take their time. They want to run out of there and jump in the car and make a getaway before you get to them.

But they need what you have to sell. That's really why they're there. So they stay. But they're still scared, because they've been told what kind of people we are. Let's face it: Salesmen don't have the best reputations in the world, because everybody tells everybody else that they are trying to take too much of your money from you. Everybody knows somebody who can get it for you cheaper or wholesale. That's one of the biggest problems in the car business, and everywhere else too. They all think they know that they are not going to get what they want at the price they ought to be paying. And that scares them.

But there they are, coming through the door, feeling this way. Full of distrust and fear, ready to say or do anything to protect themselves from what they think you are going to try to do to them. You may even run into people who will give you a $5 or even a $10 deposit just to get out of there —and never even come back for their money. So that ought to tell you something about how they feel about the situation they have walked into.

That's why a lot of us—even me sometimes—call a person The Mooch. We think of him as some kind of strange animal who will lie and stall and take up our valuable time—it *is* valuable, and we ought never to forget that basic fact.

The Bloodless War

This means that what we do every day of our working lives is a kind of war. I mean that. It is a kind of war, because prospects often come in as enemies. They think we are trying to put something over on them, and we think they are there to waste our time. But if you leave it at that, you're in trouble. Because they will keep on feeling hostile, and so will you. There will be lies and cons on both sides. Maybe they will buy, and maybe they won't. But either way, if the hostile feelings on both sides remain in force, nobody will feel good about what happens. More important, the chances of making a sale aren't very good if the suspicion, the hostility, and the distrust show.

So what do you do? I'm not ready to go into detail on the selling process yet. I still want to focus on the basic attitudes of customers and salespeople in this selling war. Let's forget

about people who really are mooches (and there are some
people for whom shopping and not buying is a kind of a
game). And let's forget about people who call themselves
salesmen but are out to screw everybody they can find because they can't handle their own emotional problems. (We
all have emotional problems sometimes, but we'll get to the
serious business of leaving them at home or converting them
into useful selling attitudes.) We're talking about people who
consider themselves serious and dedicated professional salesmen.

Now let's look at these mooches again. First of all, they
aren't mooches. They are human beings who work hard for
their money and are genuinely interested in buying something
from you. That has got to be the first basic assumption about
everybody you meet. As I have said, and as you know when
you think about it, they are scared of you, and especially of
what they are about to do. They are at war with you, and
whether you think so or not, that means you are at war with
them.

I am not saying that this is a good attitude, but I am saying
that it is generally a fact. But it is a fact that you can deal
with and turn to everybody's advantage. Because if you
understand what is going through that customer's head, you
can win that war and turn it into a valuable experience for
both you and your customer. You can do that by overcoming
your customer's initial fear and scoring a victory, that is,
making a sale.

There is no harm in thinking that a selling situation is like
a war as long as you understand that the victory—the moment
when you get the signature, the money, the sale—is an experience that is good for both sides. You have defeated an
enemy, you have scored, you have won, you have used your
time well and made money.

But the enemy, The Mooch, the scared customer, if properly
sold, has also benefited. He has got what he came in for: he
now owns the shoes or the suit or the car. He won too. And

he should feel that way. He should feel that he has spent his time well, that he has spent his money well. He has lost the war, but he has won too.

That is certainly the best kind of war—where everybody wins and nobody loses. The selling situation, if handled properly, is as good a way as any for a professional salesman to get rid of his own hostility, wherever it comes from.

I often think that every time I face a customer, I am in some way facing my father again. Now what I really have always wanted to do with my father is defeat him and make him respect and love me for doing it. In a way, I beat him every time I make a sale, which is often. But, at the same time, I have made him happy because he has bought a car from me. I don't know what a head shrinker would say about something like that. But we all have feelings of anger and fear, and if we can get over them one or two or twenty times a day by making a good sale, what's wrong with that?

And there is nothing in the professional life of a salesman that is more satisfying than making a good sale. For me, a good sale is one where the customer goes out with what he came in for, at a good enough price so that he tells his friends, his relatives, and his co-workers to buy a car from Joe Girard. That is the kind of victory I look for every day in the war against the mooches. They aren't mooches when they leave me. They are human beings who aren't afraid of me any more because we have *both* won the War of the Sale.

I have talked to people around the country who say that salespeople exploit their customers. You know what I tell them? I say: How can it be exploiting a guy when I give him a good product for his money, at a good price? And if he doesn't have the money in his pocket—and most people obviously don't—I help him get the credit to buy his car. Is that exploiting the working class, when a man leaves me owning a $5,000 automobile? I don't think so, and I'm sure you don't either.

So remember: The customer is not The Mooch when he

leaves, whatever he was when he came in. Make him a friend and he'll work for you. About 6 out of every 10 customers I sell are either an old customer coming back or somebody who got my name somewhere. That's 60 percent of all my business. Somebody who calls himself a salesman may hustle and con a customer to buy, but that guy is not going to come back to that place again if he feels he has been conned. And 60 percent of my business comes from satisfied customers and the people they know. So clean out all those expressions like The Mooch from your head. They only get in the way of seeing the real opportunities and using them.

After all, what it's all about is a satisfying way to make a good buck. And nothing is more satisfying on the job than winning and profiting. So look into your own feelings the next time you confront a customer. Try to sort out your own feelings about him. Are you sore because he interrupted a joke you were telling? Does he remind you of somebody you don't like? What if he is smoking a pipe? Forget about all that crap the other guys tell you about pipesmokers not being able to make up their minds. Maybe they do hide behind their pipes. But your job is to get them over their desire to hide from you. That's the first thing you have to do, because you can't sell a scared person. He'll run away from you. You can't sell a mooch, because he'll pick up how you feel about him. You can't sell a mooch—you can only sell a human being. So start out every encounter with everybody keeping that thought in mind. You've got a war on your hands—with your customer and with your own feelings. Don't forget who you are, and who the customer is. Don't forget why you're both there—to make a sale that is good for both of you.

You can't sell a mooch—You can only sell another human being.

5

Girard's Law of 250

I have a very strict rule about dealing with customers. In the last chapter, I tried to give you some idea of my attitude toward everybody I meet. You might think that because I am a superstar in this business I can afford to throw a guy out if he is giving me a hard time, or if I don't like his looks, or for no reason at all. Look at my sales and income record.

But if you believe that, you are missing the most important point. And that is: However I feel about myself or whoever I'm with, I don't let my feelings get in the way. This is a business we're in, an important profession. And those people, those prospects, those customers are the most important thing in the world to us, to each of us. They aren't interruptions or pains in the ass. They are what we live on. And if we don't realize that, as a hard business fact, then we don't know what we are doing. I'm not talking about some of them or most of them. I'm talking about *all* of them.

Let me explain to you what I call Girard's Law of 250.

A short time after I got into this business, I went to a funeral home to pay my last respects to the dead mother of a friend of mine. At Catholic funeral homes, they give out mass cards with the name and picture of the departed. I've seen them for years, but I never thought about them till that day. One question came into my head, so I asked the undertaker, "How do you know how many of these to print?" He said, "It's a matter of experience. You look in the book where people sign their names, and you count, and after a while you see that the average number of people who come is 250."

A short time later, a Protestant funeral director bought a car from me. After the close, I asked him the average number of people who came to see a body and attend the funeral. He said, "About 250." Then one day, my wife and I were at a wedding, and I met the man who owns the catering place where the reception took place. I asked him what the average number of guests at a wedding was, and he told me, "About 250 from the bride's side and about 250 from the groom's."

I guess you can figure out what Girard's Law of 250 is, but I'll tell you anyway: Everyone knows 250 people in his or her life important enough to invite to the wedding and to the funeral—250!

You can argue that hermits don't have that many friends, but I'll tell you that a lot of people have more than that. But the figures prove that 250 is the average. This means that if I see 50 people in a week, and only two of them are unhappy with the way I treat them, at the end of the year there will be about 5,000 people influenced by just those two a week. I've been selling cars for 14 years. So if I turned off just two people a week out of all that I see, there would be 70,000 people, a whole stadium full, who know one thing for sure: Don't buy a car from Joe Girard!

It doesn't take a mathematical genius to know that Girard's Law of 250 is the most important thing you can learn from me.

Just think about it: A guy comes in and you're feeling lousy, so you treat him lousy. He goes back to the office and somebody says, "What's the matter?" And he answers, "I just got the brushoff from Sam Glotz." Or somebody is looking to buy a car, and he hears about it and says, "Stay away from Sam Glotz. He's a baddie."

You don't know who is a shop steward or a supervisor that a lot of people in a factory or office consider a big authority. You never know that some guy is the president of his lodge and he is going from you to his lodge meeting. Or think about a barber or a dentist, people who talk to a lot of people every day as part of their work. Or another salesman of a different product.

If the average person has 250 people he sees regularly during his life, what about these other people who see a lot more than that in a week in the ordinary course of their business?

Can you afford to have just one person come to see you and leave sore and unsatisfied? Not if just an average person influences 250 others in the course of his or her life. Not if a lot of the people you deal with every day deal with a lot of other people every day.

People talk a lot to other people about what they buy and what they plan to buy. Others are always offering advice about where to buy what and how much to pay. That's a big part of the everyday life of ordinary people.

Can you afford to jeopardize just one of those people? I can't. And you know that if anyone can afford to, I can. But I know I can't, because I know how much of my sales and my income comes from people telling other people about me. It's a powerful force in my professional life, and it should be in yours.

We are not talking about love or friendship. We are talking about business. I don't care what you really think of the people you deal with. It's the way you act toward them, the way you deal with them, that is the only important thing. Of course, if you can't control your real feelings, then you've got a problem. But this is business, and in business all of these people—the mooches, the flakes, the finks, the pipesmokers —can be money in your pocket.

But when you turn away one, just one, with anger or a smart-ass remark, you are running the risk of getting a bad name among at least 250 other people with money in their pockets who might want to give some of it to you.

This is a businesslike attitude that you had better develop and keep in your head every working hour of every day, if you don't want to be wiped out by Girard's Law of 250.

Every time you turn off just one prospect, you turn off 250 more.

6
Don't Join
the Club

I didn't discover the Law of 250 on my first day as a salesman. It took me a few years to work it out. I can't guess how much it cost me in lost customers and their friends and relatives and co-workers. I have to admit that even in recent years I have blown it once in a while when somebody makes a remark about "dagos" or "wops." But sometimes my efforts to cool my hot Sicilian blood don't work.

I did learn one important lesson very early in my career: *Don't join the club.* Most salesmen learn it on their first day in a new place but soon forget it. What it means is this: Don't become a part of what we call the "dope ring" or the "bull ring" in the place where you work. That is where all the guys get together in the morning and spend their time discussing what they did last night, or what their wife was complaining about at breakfast, or some other subject that has nothing to do with work.

Everybody knows what I'm talking about. A salesman comes

up to the crowd and says, "Did you hear about Phil Jones?" Phil Jones was a guy that worked there ten years ago and nobody knows him, but they listen as he tells about how Phil had an accident or won the lottery. What for? How much money does that make you?

Then the coffee wagon comes around and everybody starts flipping quarters to see whose turn it is to pay this morning. The day is going by, and pretty soon it's getting toward lunch time. Now the question is: Where are we gonna eat? Somebody mentions a place, and then they argue and take a vote and finally they go to lunch, usually at a place where other salesmen go, so they're not likely to meet anybody who can help them earn a nickel. After lunch, there is more time lost with stories and talk about who owes whom how much for the meal. Before long the day is gone, and so is any chance to build your business.

Remember: It is *your* business, no matter whom you work for or what you sell. And the better you build it, the more the people you sell become *your* customers. Every minute you spend looking for ways to avoid working costs you money. You want to tell me you've heard that before? But if you are part of that clubby group of salesmen hanging around the front door, you are not using what you know, because you can't make money hanging out with the boys.

Learn from Your Own Experience

I said that you already know that, if you have been a professional salesman for any length of time. All you have to do is think back to the time you first came to work at your present place of employment. Remember when you didn't know any of the guys. You felt a little lonely. There was nobody to talk to. So you had to look for things to do. Maybe you spent a little time getting to know the merchandise. Maybe you tried to edge up near where the top man was talking to a customer so you could learn something about the way he did it. Maybe you even worked the telephone or sent out some pieces of direct mail to friends and relatives to tell them where you were working and what you were selling. Nobody had to tell you to do those things because if you have any business sense, you know those are things a salesman has got to do when he starts working at a new place. It's like a grand opening.

More important, you did those things because you had plenty of spare time. There was nobody to talk to, nobody to buddy up to. Then, after a while, you become one of the boys and stop doing most or all of that sort of thing. You aren't the hot shot any more and you wonder what happened to that business you were doing when you first got there. Well, that's the way it goes, you say to yourself. Sometimes you're hot and sometimes you're not.

The Thrill of Victory

Don't believe it. Very early in my own career, I learned that lesson the hard way. Once I had nailed that bag of groceries to feed my family, I understood the value of a selling victory. First of all, there was that immediate want: To bring home food. But there was something more than that, because in that first sale there was the special thrill of making a sale itself. I had sold a few houses a year back in my days as a builder. But they did not take much real selling at the price I was asking and in those days of scarce, cheap houses. But getting that Coca-Cola salesman to buy a Chevrolet from me was a real triumph. Not only did I get the groceries and my commission, but I felt the excitement of the victory that every salesman experiences if he is a real salesman. That was my first sale, and it gave me the confidence to try everything I could think of to rack up a lot more. I didn't know any of the other salesmen there, and I knew that they resented a new face because they saw me as somebody there to take away business from them. So I didn't make any friends. Instead, I sold a lot of cars. In my first month I sold 13, and in my second month I sold 18. I was among the very top performers in that dealership at the end of my second month. Then I got fired.

It's been a long time since that happened, but what I remember was that the other guys objected to my sales. They claimed that I was taking business away from them. What they really were objecting to, I think, was that I was a new guy with no past experience, and I was doing as well or better than they were. Also I wasn't very friendly to them.

So I went to work at another dealership where I have been ever since. When I first got there, the sales manager told me that I'd do better if I didn't spend the time on the floor being pals with the other salesmen. I had already begun to learn that, but I also knew that there was no point in making enemies of them. So I've tried to be careful about that ever since. They know that I operate differently from the way they do, and that I don't like to waste my days in the dope ring. And they know that it pays off for me. There are the usual rough edges between people working in the same place. But I have managed to work *my* way and still stay in the same place.

Among the favorite topics of conversation of salesmen in my business are which dealership is best, what's wrong with the place they're working at, and how it's better somewhere else where their friend works. But I have stayed in the same place all these years because what counts most is *how* you work, not *where* you work. We have a good location, but so do most Chevrolet dealers, or any good dealers, for that matter. And our pay plan is about as good as any other. So I have found that what counts most is how smart I work, which is even more important than how hard I work.

When the rest of the guys go to lunch, they know that I hardly ever will go along with them, because I have other things to do. When I go to lunch with somebody, it is for good business reasons, not just to be a good fellow. I'll discuss whom I take to lunch, what I do, and why in another chapter. But just let me say right now that I'm all business when I'm working, whatever it *seems* like.

The message I'm trying to get across is this: *Don't join the club*. And if you are in it, ease your way out, because it will encourage other bad habits and wrong attitudes.

Think of this: How many times, when the sales manager has called a sales meeting, do you hear all the guys groan and say, "Here comes another crap session"? When I started selling cars, I didn't know anything about selling cars or selling anything else. I went to the meetings because I figured I might learn something. And you know what? I did learn. You may not like your sales manager, but he probably knows a lot about selling. Though I'll agree that most of the films they show us are not very good. That's because they are mostly made by people who have never actually sold anything except films. (That's why I make and sell my own sales training films: because, even though mine aren't as slick looking, companies who buy them tell me that mine look and feel right about selling.) Even so, the stuff that the manager would tell us at sales meetings made sense to me. And I figured that he knew more about selling than I did, which was true in those days at least. And I found that if I did what he and those films said, it would work and I would get more business. Whatever it was, using the telephone, sending out direct mail, anything, would work if I did it a lot.

Later on, I learned to do things even better my own way and even made up my own direct mail pieces, which worked better for me than theirs did. But what they had to say and what they told us to do was better than nothing. A lot better than nothing, and that is something you may not learn if you join the club. Because hardly anybody who hangs out with the boys all day is going to tell you how much business you can get just by using the telephone for an hour or even

10 minutes a day. And none of your buddies is going to say, "Don't listen to my stupid joke. Go to your desk and write names and addresses on 10 pieces of direct mail and send them out every day and you will be in touch with 2,500 people every year who drive cars and will need another one some day."

Most of the guys in the club think that all the business you will need walks in the door every day. So they will never tell you what I know: That you can build the biggest business in town without being in the club, because you can spend all your time getting people to come and ask for *you,* and not just walk in the door and wait for the guy who is up. A lot of salesmen do fairly well that way, as long as their luck holds out. But nobody can sell everybody. So the salesman who waits his turn has to take his chances.

Stacking the Odds in Your Favor

I don't like to take chances in my work. When I go to Las Vegas, I know what the odds are, and if I want to take chances, well, that's what I'm there for. But I don't like to gamble with my working life and the security of my family, so I don't take chances in my work. I *make* my opportunities. And one of the most important ways to do that is to stay out of the club.

In my neighborhood, we used to have an expression: If you throw enough spaghetti against the wall, some of it has got to stick. Maybe the Chinese talk about throwing rice against the wall. But, however you look at it, that is the basic law of probabilities in our business. That's a lot different from just standing there with the boys and taking the luck of the draw.

That means if you do a lot of things to build business, you'll build business. They don't have to be done perfectly to work —although the better you do them, the better they'll work. But the main point is that you have to do them—a lot. And you can't do what has to be done to turn the odds in your favor, unless you stay out of the club.

O.K., you ask, but what do you do to get it started? You can do a lot of different things. We'll get to them, and you can pretty much pick what works best for you, what fits your style, your personality, your interests. But the trick is to do *something*. I've talked to a lot of people over the years in a lot of different types of selling. They all pretty much agree that there is a lot of turnover among beginning salespeople. And the reason that is true is because just about anybody can make a few sales at the start. Whether it is cars or insurance or anything else, everybody can buy one himself, sell one to his father-in-law, and sell another one to his best friend. "After the third sale," a sales manager once told me, "is when you know if a guy is a real salesman or not."

What do you do after you have sold those easy ones, the people who buy because they want to help you? That is the big question, and that's what we turn to now.

Don't join the club. Instead use all your time to make opportunities.

7

What Do You Do
After You Sell
Your Uncle Harry?

I didn't have an Uncle Harry or a mother-in-law who could afford to buy a car because I needed to sell one. And, as I have already made pretty clear, I sure needed to sell one. But I had that Coca-Cola guy, thank you wherever you are. And then I had that prospect list I told you about. Four pages from the Detroit phone book—two white, two yellow. And there was a telephone on my desk. I was new and green and didn't know that the only way to sell was to stand around matching quarters and stories until it was my turn—my "up" —to take a shot at somebody walking through the front door. I had promised I would not take floor time from the other salesmen, and mostly I kept my promise. And I worked my list. You don't believe I worked a list made out of pages from the phone book? Well, I've got news for you: I did it. And I'll bet you anything that if I had to, I could do it today and make a good living.

It is easy to argue that cold contact calls guarantee a lot of useless work. That's true. You get a lot of no answers, some out-of-service numbers, a few people who don't understand you, and some who don't speak English. But if you work it right, you get some action. And if you have a few dead minutes or an unfilled hour, you can afford the hard physical labor of making half a dozen phone calls to get nothing, and maybe just one that gives you a live lead. All that effort may turn out to be a little more valuable than scratching your nose or listening to a bad joke.

There are a lot of more productive ways to get leads than cold telephone calls. But if you have nothing better to do, this kind of call is worth a try. We will get to the ways to develop a system for getting leads, prospects, and customers soon enough. But right now I want to prove to you that even this least productive way of getting business—cold calls from the phone book—is better than doing nothing.

So pick up the phone, even if you don't have a good list of prospects. If you are located in a suburban area that has a separate phone book or a separate section for your part of town, that's better, of course. But it isn't necessary. Remember, I did it with pages torn out of the book at random. If I had to do it that way today, I'd thumb through for a few minutes, looking at street addresses or names that sounded right. And then I'd pick up the phone.

How to Sell on the Phone

Let's say I hit 10 duds in a row: don't answers, no speak English, Mommy went shopping. Now I'm calling during the daytime, so I don't want to call too early. It's late morning. But suppose I get nothing at all on my first 10 calls. What has it cost me? Three or four minutes? O.K. Now a woman answers the phone. "Hello, Mrs. Kowalski. This is Joe Girard at Merollis Chevrolet. I just wanted to let you know that the car you ordered is ready," I tell her. Now remember: This is a cold call, and all I know for sure from the phone book is the party's name, address, and phone number. This Mrs. Kowalski doesn't know what I'm talking about. "I'm afraid you have the wrong number. We haven't ordered a new car," she tells me. "Are you sure?" I ask. "Pretty sure. My husband would have told me," she says. "Just a minute," I say. "Is this the home of Clarence J. Kowalski?" "No. My husband's name is Steven." I write it down, though of course I know it because it says so right there in the phone book. "Gee, Mrs. Kowalski, I'm very sorry to have disturbed you at this hour of the day. I'm sure you're very busy." Maybe she says it's no trouble at all or wants to tell me that she just got back from the supermarket. Whatever it is, I don't let her hang up yet.

I want to keep her on the phone, because I'm not done, and maybe she has no one to talk to so she doesn't hang up. "Mrs. Kowalski, you don't happen to be in the market for a new car, do you?" If she knows they are, she'll probably say yes. But the typical answer will be: "I don't think so, but you'd have to ask my husband." There it is, what I'm looking for. "Oh, when can I reach him?" And she'll say, "He's usually home by six." O.K., I've got what I wanted. "Well, fine, Mrs. Kowalski, I'll call back then, if you're sure I won't be interrupting supper." I wait for her to tell me they don't eat until about six-thirty, and then I thank her.

You know what I am going to be doing at six o'clock. That's right. "Hello, Mr. Kowalski, this is Joe Girard at Merollis Chevrolet. I spoke to Mrs. Kowalski this morning and she suggested I call back at this time. I was wondering if you're in the market for a new Chevrolet?" "No," he says, "not just yet." So I ask, "Well, when do you think you might start looking at a new car?" I ask that question straight out, and he is going to think about it and give me an answer. Maybe he only wants to get rid of me. But whatever the reason, what he says is probably going to be what he really means. It's easier than trying to dream up a lie. "I guess I'll be needing one in about six months," he says, and I finish with: "Fine, Mr. Kowalski, I'll be getting in touch with you then. Oh, by the way, what are you driving now?" He tells me, I thank him, and hang up.

I also write down his name, address, and phone number, along with whatever information I have picked up in the conversation such as where he works, how many kids they have, and what he drives. I put it all on a three-by-five card for my file and my mailing list, and I also write it down in a diary that I keep. I write it down alongside six o'clock on a day about five months from now—not six, like he said. When that date comes up, you better believe I will call him up and do everything I can to get him in to buy that car he told me he is going to need then.

This is priceless information I developed from a two-minute telephone conversation. Selling is an espionage game. If you want to sell something to someone, you should find out all you can about that person that pertains to your business. If you're selling typewriters to businesses, you could find out from the company receptionist how many typewriters they have, how old they are, how often they are in need of repair, what kind they are, does the company own or lease them, is the company growing, will they be hiring new secretaries, who the decision maker is. No matter what you sell, if you'll spend some time each day filling the seats on the Ferris wheel you will soon have a line of people waiting to be sold.

Making Your Own Prospect Lists

When I started out, I just put this stuff on a piece of paper and shoved it into a drawer. But one day I discovered a lead that I hadn't followed because I didn't have a system. So I went to a stationery store and bought a diary and a little three-by-five card file. That was the beginning of my intelligence system. I transferred everything on all those scraps of paper into my records system, and I had the start of a mailing list and a telephone call-back system. If you don't have anything like that, you had better get one, because you can't possibly keep all the leads you can develop in your head or on the backs of envelopes in your pocket, not if you are doing a proper job of prospecting.

I just described a cold call that got me a good lead and eventually a sale. That happened not just once, but many times, I can't count how many times. And chances are I've sold a lot of people named Kowalski. So even the name wasn't complete fiction.

Now you'll have to admit that what I did is not magic. It isn't even very hard to do. In fact, you have probably heard and seen other people make cold telephone calls that worked pretty much the way mine did. So I don't really need to tell you much more about this technique. But we all have to be reminded to do these obvious, easy things instead of hanging out with the boys.

As I have said, I don't particularly enjoy the buddy-buddy bull sessions in the showroom. I find them a waste of valuable selling time. And besides, I can always think of something else more important to do than hang around doing nothing. I like the money I make, and I like the thrill of closing a deal. In fact, you might say I am a selling junkie. I love the kick of getting a sale. But it soon wears off, so I have to do it again and again and again. I get bad withdrawal symptoms if I don't sell cars every day, a lot of them. So sometimes I sell as many cars in a week as other guys sell in a month. If they're satisfied with that kind of performance, that's their business. But I'm not, and I do something, a lot of things, about it.

Let's face this fact: If somebody can sell five cars a week just by hanging around and taking his turns at the door, he knows how to sell. But if he can do that, think of what he can do if he can build five times as much traffic coming in just to see him. If he is just as effective in closing this extra business, his earnings will zoom, even if he only gets the same percentage of sales as he got before.

So what you do after you sell your Uncle Harry is build up the flow, and get all the seats filled on the Ferris wheel. There are plenty of ways to do that. Cold calling is one. But there are other ways, and as you work at it, you will see that the other ways are even more productive, better ways to fill your time, so that you can feel the thrill of selling, and make big money getting your kicks.

After the easy ones, there are many Kowalskis, if you keep searching.

8

Fill the Seats on the Ferris Wheel

In an earlier chapter, I said that good selling is like planting and harvesting in a country where things grow all year round. Planting and harvesting, all year long. Another way to think of it is in terms of the Ferris wheel that I just mentioned. If you have ever seen a Ferris wheel, you know how it works. One at a time, the guy in charge fills the seats. People get off, he fills their seats, moves the wheel a little, fills the next seats, and so on until all the people in the seats have left and new ones come on. Then the wheel turns a while and he stops it and does that emptying and filling again.

Good selling is like that too. Only the wheel is always moving just a little bit so that some people—the ones you have just sold—can get off for a while and others—the ones you are just starting to work on—can get on. By the time they have come full circle, they are ready to be sold, give up their seats, and be replaced for a while. I say "for a while," because nobody buys a car forever. People buy one for two or three or maybe five years and then they are ready for another one, whether they know it or not. But if you keep proper records and files and diaries, *you* know it, maybe even before *they* do.

In my example in the last chapter, I put Steve Kowalski in a seat on the Ferris wheel. In a way, I have him locked in that seat. I know what he drives, so I know he probably will want to trade. I know something about the age of his car, so I'll know a little about how much money he will need to have or borrow to buy a new one. I know where he lives and maybe where he works, so I have an idea of how good a credit risk he is and where he is likely to go for borrowing: a credit union, a small loan company, or whatever. And I know when he thinks he will start looking for a new car, and I'll be back on the phone a few weeks before he says he'll start looking. So I'll probably be ahead of the other salesmen he is likely to see. In fact, if I handle it right, I may be the only salesman he ever talks to. He is sitting up there on my wheel, and I know exactly where.

A lot of the time, let's face it, it doesn't work quite that way. Sometimes a guy won't tell you that much. Or maybe you don't even know who is up there on your wheel, because you sent somebody a piece of mail and he put it aside, and you don't even know it.

That doesn't really matter. I mean it is great to get a Steve Kowalski, a good prospect, already partly qualified, just from a couple of phone calls. But don't forget the spaghetti throwing. You get it out there and some of it will stick. Maybe when I call Kowalski back, he will have won the lottery and bought a Rolls Royce already. So what? I ask him if he knows anybody else who is looking to buy a car—a relative who was over for dinner, somebody in his shop, maybe a neighbor who totaled his car yesterday. Or maybe I just wish him luck and let him tell me about where he bought the lottery ticket. Then I suggest that it might be nice to use some of that money to buy his wife or his daughter who is graduating a new car too. Or maybe I just make some pleasant small talk and he remembers me when he has blown all the money and needs a cheap car again.

I may or may not know exactly where Steve Kowalski is sitting. But I do know his name and where to reach him and when. And that is worth something. It is a piece of information that can be mined like you're looking for gold. He is worth calling back, maybe more than once, and he is worth putting on a mailing list and being in touch with again.

When I talk about this guy, I'm sure you understand that I am really referring to a lot of people—the more, the better. I have sold more than 12,000 cars and trucks since I got into the automobile business. Since I have an increasing volume of repeat business, it is hard to say how many of those 12,000 plus sales are repeats. It is all written down in my records. I have a card for every buyer, and if I sold a person more than once it says when and what and all the rest. So let's say that there are 9,000 different names of sold customers in my file.

You would think that mailing to 9,000 names is an expensive proposition, and it is. After all, if I mail them all first class, it costs plenty for postage alone these days. But my mailing list is bigger than that, because it also includes names of people I have not sold yet. So it costs me a lot to keep those records and do the mailings. The dealer pays a good part of the cost, but I pay plenty too. But it's worth it, every penny of the cost of maintaining the list and keeping it up-to-date, to say nothing of the mailings themselves.

If you had a list like that, you would understand its value. That many names of solid prospects is the most valuable thing a salesman can have. Maybe you won't be able to put together anywhere near that many names. It doesn't matter, because however big your prospect list is, it is a list of people you have already qualified in some way.

There are millions of prospects in the whole country and maybe a few hundred thousand in any major metropolitan area. But getting your hands on the specifics—name, address, anything else—of real people is enormously valuable. I don't have to tell you that. But I just want to remind you in case you are falling into the habit of moaning about how nobody comes to see you.

You Already Have a Long Prospect List

What are you doing to bring them in? Who? you ask. Well, for openers, do all your friends and relatives know where you are working these days? You've got a little address book in your pocket with their names. That's a prospect list that I'm sure you already know about. But what have you done lately to be in touch with them?

Here's another good source of prospects: your file of paid bills. What I am saying is that the people you buy things from ought to be good prospects for the things you sell. Everybody wears clothes, lives in a house or apartment with furniture and appliances, drives a car. And businessmen—like the butcher and the florist and the oil dealer—use trucks. All the people I buy from are on my list. I try to sell them every time I see them to buy from them. When I give them money, I let them know again what I sell. And I work it the other way too. If a guy buys a car from me, I know what business he is in. When I need some of what he sells, I will buy some from him, and let him know that I appreciate his buying from me. I'm not saying we can all live by taking in each other's laundry. But the people you buy from certainly ought to be on your prospect list. So check back into your personal bills file to see whom you're giving your money to. Maybe it's time they gave some to you.

Girard's Law of 250 is *always* operating. And when we are talking about your butcher and your filling station and your dry cleaner, figure that they talk to that many people in a day sometimes. Every one of these people talks to customers, hears small talk about kids and accidents and cars. Some of them may not even know what you do for a living, so you ought to make sure that they do know.

Make Sure Everybody Knows What You Sell

That sounds like pretty elementary advice, and maybe you've heard it too many times already. But I have run into a lot of salesmen who never tell people—other than close friends and relatives—what they do for a living. They say that sales people, especially car salesmen, have a bad image. Well, let me tell you that I'm proud of what I do for a living.

If your sales are to business or industry, you may think this isn't important or that it can't help you. I say it can. Remember Girard's Law of 250. People are always talking about who they know and what they do. I know of a salesman who sold a $120,000 computer service because a friend told another friend about him.

I believe that every salesperson ought to be proud of his or her profession. Look at it this way. Since I was 35 years old, I have sold more than 12,000 new cars and trucks. Do you know how many jobs that has created, how much steel had to be produced and sold to make those cars, how much money General Motors and all of its thousands of suppliers took in just from what I did? Millions. Salesmen make the wheels go round, because if we don't keep on moving the goods off the shelves and out of the stockrooms and warehouses, the whole American system would stop running.

So you make sure everybody knows you're a salesman and that they know what you sell. And when you buy from them, you don't have to make some kind of trade with them, some kind of reciprocal deal. But just let them know every once in a while that you have something for them any time they need it. And what you want from them is not just a sale but information. If you sell jewelry, when you hear that somebody is going to graduate, you know that can be a lead to a sale of a watch or a cocktail ring. And if you are selling cars, when you hear that a guy totaled his car, you can say you're sorry, but also keep in mind that this guy is going to need another car and that he is probably going to get a nice big check from an insurance company to pay for it.

So don't forget about the butcher and the baker. They can help you fill those seats on the Ferris wheel or plant those seeds in the fertile soil, or however you want to look at what I consider the professional system of selling.

Now let's get specific about some of my other methods for getting those seats filled or seeds planted or spaghetti stuck on the wall. However you look at it, it is going to be the way to get money in your pocket.

Put everybody you can think of on your Ferris wheel.

9

Girard's Toolbox

If I had to name the tools that work best to build my business, the list would probably not surprise you by this time. It would obviously include the telephone, my files, the mail, my business cards, and my birddogs.

I've already told you how the phone can be used profitably with cold calls. If you never did anything else but that, you could build yourself a good business, as I demonstrated. And I've said something about the way I keep my records. I use a diary to remind me when to call back long-term prospects, whether I get them from cold calls or from any other method. But let's face it: Satisfied customers are the best bet for future sales. That's why I guard my card file of customers practically with my life. I keep two sets of those cards, one at my office at the dealership and the other off the premises. And I keep both sets of cards in fireproof cabinets, which cost $375 apiece. But they are worth far more than that to me. There is no way I could ever get all that information together again if anything happened to my files. That's why I keep two sets, even though they are in vaults.

Start Building Your File Now

When you make your own card file, put down everything you notice about a customer or a prospect. I mean everything: kids, hobbies, travels, whatever you learn about the person, because they give you ways to talk to the prospective customer about things in which he is interested. And that means you can disarm him by leading him into subjects that take his mind off what you are trying to do, which of course is to trade him your product for his money.

There is nothing more effective in selling anything than getting the customer to believe, really believe, that you like him and care about him. The selling situation is, as I have said, a contest, even a kind of war. But that doesn't mean that you should let the prospect know this. In fact, the opposite is what you should be doing. You want him to relax, to unwind, and to trust you. That is why I strongly recommend that you keep in your files all the small bits of information you can pick up from him and about him. Later on, we'll get to the whole subject of handling people once you get them to come in. But right now I want to keep focusing on the process of getting them in.

I'll mention mail briefly here. It is a subject that is very important to my business, and it should be to yours. It deserves a separate chapter, and it will get one. But right now I want to mention briefly some of the occasions and methods that anybody can use to build business. Obviously, if you happen to know the birthday of a customer, his wife, and his kids, you will have them in your prospect file. You can imagine the impact if you send them birthday cards. If you're selling anything more valuable than groceries or neckties, the cost of doing that will be more than paid for by the way it reminds them of you in the most favorable light.

Personalized mail is the best thing that anybody can receive from a salesperson. Some clothing salesmen will send their customers flyers that manufacturers put out for new coats or suits. Now just think of the impact if you write a little note on the side that says: "I'm holding a 42 regular for you, so please stop by soon and try it on." You obligate a prospect at least to call and tell you he doesn't want *that* one. Then you have a shot at getting him in to sell him something else. Or at least to let him know you're thinking about him specifically.

In the car business, direct mail is a regular part of the selling process. The manufacturers provide it, and the dealers pay part or all of the cost of mailing it out. I used factory pieces for years, and I think they are pretty good, certainly a lot better than nothing. But in a later chapter I am going to describe my own personal direct mail program. You can take off from it and develop one of your own. Or at least you will get some ideas on how to make your own mail contacts with your prospects more effective.

A Small but Powerful Selling Tool

Just about every salesman has business cards. But I know a lot of them who don't go through a box of 500 in a year. I go through that many in a good week.

If I had to pick one thing to get business, I would have a very hard time doing it. But if I really had to make that almost impossible choice, I would probably pick my business card. But it is not just an ordinary card that the dealer has printed, with the salesman's name down in a corner, or at least not featured prominently. My card is distinctively my own. It even has my picture on it. Of course I pay the extra cost of printing. But so what! It's a valuable tool to me. I use it constantly, and in my tax bracket, nothing I pay out for business purposes costs me more than half price, because I'd pay that much in taxes anyway.

Even today, though, the cost of printing distinctive calling cards is low. And it is certainly money well spent. I hand them out wherever I am. I even leave them with the money when I pay the check in restaurants. Almost everybody drives a car, so every waiter or waitress is a prospect, especially when I leave my card with a little larger than normal tip. Nothing lavish and crazy. You don't want people to think you are too wealthy, because they may get the idea that you don't need their business. But suppose your check is $20 for a meal. The normal 15 percent tip would be $3. I will usually leave $4 and my card. Then they remember Joe Girard.

I have even been known to throw cards out by the handful during big moments at sports events. At a football game, everybody gets up to watch a touchdown scored, and while they are hollering and waving and cheering, so am I. Only I am also throwing out bunches of my cards, which I brought along in a paper bag. So maybe I am littering the stadium. But if at least one of the hundred cards gets into somebody's hands who needs a car or knows somebody who does, I've made enough commission to make the day worthwhile.

You may think that this is strange behavior, but I am certain that it has got me some sales. I have also started a lot of interest in buying from me, because throwing cards is an unusual thing to do, and people don't forget things like that. The point is that wherever there are people, there are prospects, and if you let them know you are there and what you do, you are building your business.

Try to Sell Everybody You Talk To

A lot of you probably don't remember the days after World War II when the Hudson car was still around. Well, even in those days of shortages when practically anything with four wheels took months, even years, to get, the Hudson was a dog that you could hardly give away. So one day I meet this guy in Las Vegas and we start talking and it turns out that he is a very rich man who had been a car dealer until he made so much money that he retired. What did you sell? I asked him. Hudsons. I couldn't believe it.

He told me how he did it. He had a rule that he followed and made everybody who worked for him stick to—not only salesmen but mechanics and the office help and everybody else. Every time he met someone or talked to someone on the telephone, he would ask one question before he did or said anything else: "Would you like to buy a car now, without waiting?" That was the rule, and that was the way he built his big business selling a car that nobody else could sell.

It's like passing out cards to everybody you meet or do business with. Somebody needs a car, and your card can get handed around a lot until finally it gets to somebody who is in the market at that moment. And there is your sale. What do cards cost? Practically nothing. Say $9 a thousand. But if you get only one sale for every thousand cards you pass out, the cost doesn't mean a thing, because the odds are overwhelmingly on your side. Effective use of business cards—which means carrying bunches of them all the time and giving them out everywhere—is one of the cheapest business building tools you can have.

Besides all the ways I have mentioned of spreading them around, I use them in my birddog system, which is the subject of another chapter. But let me just tie together some points I have already made. Girard's Law of 250 tells you what happens when you turn somebody against you. But, even more important, it tells you what happens when you make a friend, a booster, a satisfied customer. Now put that together with 250 people, each with your card in his pocket. You can see what happens if they don't do anything else but pull one out of their pockets once in a while by accident.

O.K., but business is not love—it is money. Now suppose that every one of these 250 people who like you and have your card also have an incentive to get other people to buy from you—an incentive like money or a free dinner or free service. That is basically what I mean when I talk about birddogs. You can figure out a lot of ways of putting that combination together yourself to build winners. But we're going to talk about the ways I have built my birddog system to the point where it produces maybe 550 car sales for me every year at a very small out-of-pocket cost.

If you have a telephone, a mailbox, a pen, a file of prospects, and business cards, you have the most valuable tools in the world for doing business. You may know others that I don't know. I am always willing to admit that I don't know all there is to know about selling. But I will not admit that anybody in my business has ever done better than I have. So take my word for it when I guarantee you that the proper use of these simple tools can make you a star selling professional.

Fill your toolbox—and use it all the time.

10

Getting Them to Read the Mail

The mail may be your most important means of contacting your prospects and customers on a regular basis. But let's face it. In this day and age, with everybody and his uncle getting tons of junk mail every day, effective use of the mail can be a real challenge. I have seen apartment houses where there is a giant garbage can near the tenants' mailboxes in which they can dump all the junk mail. And most of it isn't even looked at before it is thrown away.

It used to be one of the basic rules of automobile selling that if you sent out direct mail you would get business. Now we have to add the words "and get it read" if we want this rule to mean anything. That is why I suggested, in the previous chapter, the writing of a personal note on the printed stuff. Probably your best bet, if you have to use canned material that looks like junk mail, is to write a personal message on the outside of the envelope.

Some salesmen, who used to send out material provided by

manufacturers, have given up almost entirely on mailings. They figure that it just isn't worth the bother. But they're wrong, and I can prove it.

Just stop to think of the first words that come out of the average person's mouth when he comes home after work. First he says something like "Hello, honey, how was your day to-day?" Then he says, "How are the kids (or your mother or the dog)?" And then he says, "Was there any mail?"

Think about it for a minute and you will realize that this is almost exactly what is said. And this proves that people are still very interested in a lot of what comes to them through the mail. But what they care about are the things worth look-ing at, not the junk that the wife throws out when the mailman leaves, which she doesn't even mention to her husband.

Here's the Real Game—Getting It Read

So the game today is to make sure that what you send gets opened and read and maybe kept. Practically everybody in the selling business sends his list a card every Christmas. And you know how most people receive Christmas cards. They open them, talk about who sent them and how nice, unusual, or chintzy they are, and put them on the mantel to look at and show to friends.

But you send a Christmas card only once a year. And if you don't send anything else but junk mail, you get lost in the shuffle. I don't. My mailings get opened and read and talked about, and maybe even kept for a while.

Why? For one thing, because I fool my mailing list. I don't send them things they can easily identify as advertising mail and throw away without opening. I send 12 pieces of mail a year to my customer list. And every one of those pieces is in a different color and shape envelope. They are interesting to get. Never put the name of your business on the outside of the envelope. The person doesn't know what's inside. Don't show your hand; it's like playing poker. The person wants to know what's inside and whom it's from. I guarantee you that if you got on my mailing list, you would not throw away a single piece without opening and reading it. They look like real mail, the kind you want to get, the kind that makes you curious when you take it out of the box.

What's more, when you open and read one of my pieces, you don't feel that you have been conned. You are not disappointed in what you find inside. Don't get me wrong. I don't put a $5 bill in every envelope, or in any of them. But I do put a nice, very soft-sell message in there. Very soft sell, but in this case it is the best kind of sell, because you will open it and read it and talk about it and remember it.

In January you will get a message that says: HAPPY NEW YEAR—I LIKE YOU. It has a nice piece of art work on it, appropriate to the occasion, and it is signed: "Joe Girard, Merollis Chevrolet." That is all the sell you get. Nothing about coming in to take advantage of the year-end clearance, none of that. Just HAPPY NEW YEAR—I LIKE YOU, from Joe Girard, Merollis Chevrolet. In February you get a HAPPY VALENTINE'S DAY—I LIKE YOU with the same signature. ST. PATRICK'S DAY—I LIKE YOU in March. It doesn't matter if you're black or Polish or Jewish. You still like that message and like me for sending it. One month everybody gets a HAPPY BIRTHDAY—I LIKE YOU. If it works out to be the month of your birthday, I lucked in and you are very pleased. If not, you still think it's a cute card.

The Best Time of the Month

Another thing I am careful about is not having the pieces go into the mail the same time that bills go out, which means not at the first or fifteenth. But whenever they arrive at home, when Daddy comes home and asks his question—"Was there any mail?"—the answer comes back: "Yes, there was another card from Joe Girard." My name is in that household 12 times a year in a very pleasant way. Everybody on my mailing list knows my name and what I do for a living. When it comes time for them to buy a car, I have got to be the very first person that practically every single one of those thousands of people thinks of. Not only that, but even if they hear of somebody else looking to buy a car—down at the shop or in the office— they are probably going to suggest my name.

They would probably suggest my name just from getting those pleasant holiday messages every month. But there is another, much more important reason why. That is because, at least once every year, most of the people on the list get one of my birddog recruiting kits as part of the mailing.

I am going to cover the whole birddog system in the next chapter. But at this point I'll just say that what I gave the fancy name of "birddog recruiting kit" is a mailing that includes a small stack of my business cards plus a printed reminder that I will pay the person $25 cash every time he or she sends me somebody who buys a car. And the way he (or she) is to make sure I know he sent someone in is to write his name on the back of my card that he gives to the person he sent to me. But we'll get back to that later.

Right now I want to emphasize again that mail is still a very effective way to reach prospects. But with the flood of junk mail filling the pipes, you have to make sure your pieces are getting through. I don't mean whether or not they are being delivered. I mean whether they are getting through the flood of junk, being opened and read, so that your name is spoken and remembered.

I imagine that when you just read what I said about my mailings, you probably thought: *Sure, it's fine for a big operator like Girard to talk about designing special envelopes and mailing pieces. He can afford it.* That's true, I can afford it. But you can't afford *not* to do something that will be as effective, in its way, as my stuff is.

I mean, if you are going to send out the routine stuff with third-class postage, your stuff will look like the other junk that gets thrown away. I'm not saying that nobody reads any of that stuff. But the odds are way down. Of course, if your employer pays the whole bill and lets you address the people who receive it, it may be worth something. Your name will be on it through a rubber stamp or a sticker. And that's not too bad. I don't want to knock it too much. But it is a pretty weak way to go about reaching your prospects by mail.

If you have a list of prime people worth reaching at all, the extra money you and your employer spend to be sure they notice and read your stuff has got to be worth the money. If nothing else, use plain envelopes and first-class postage, even if all you are doing is sending out routine factory-produced pieces. At least people will stop and open them and maybe see your name before they throw them in the rubbish can. That is better than nothing—a lot better, in some cases. And maybe it is all that your volume and your kind of business can support.

If They Bought Before, They're Your Best Prospects Now

But the top people on your list, the ones who have bought from you before and are satisfied with the relationship, will more than pay for the extra effort and money it takes to attract their attention. Maybe you sell appliances and radios and TVs. Say you have a list of people you have sold a couple of thousand dollars' worth of stuff to in the last five years. Not just walk-ins who bought a transistor radio, but people you sold a whole kitchen to or a $600 color TV set or $700 worth of stereo equipment for their children. Of course you have a list of those people. They gave you a lot of money. Now I know that refrigerators and stoves are bought a lot less often than cars. But there are a lot of related products that keep coming out that those people probably will be buying from somebody: microwave ovens, CB radios, electronic games that are played through TV sets, all kinds of things like that. Those people will come back to you if you keep reminding them that you exist, in a nice way.

Maybe you have only 200 or 300 of those prospects. What is it going to cost you to buy some holiday cards? Hallmark and the other big card makers have them for every holiday, including some I never heard of. A nice rubber stamp or sticker with your name and the name of the place where you sell, and you're in business. You can hand-address a list of prime prospects like that. If nothing else, you can send them cards at gift-giving times—HAPPY GRADUATION, that sort of thing. In fact, if you go into a card store and look through the racks, you might find some really right things to mail that don't cost much and would make a first-rate impression.

It may not be too subtle—if you're in the appliance, jewelry, clothing, or travel business—to send out a few cards at gift-giving times. But you don't want to be too subtle. A little sell —"Joe Girard, Merollis Chevrolet"—is all it takes. People make the connection if they like what you say. They will even like being reminded of what they can give the kid who is graduating or getting married, or of Mother's Day or whatever occasion seems appropriate to use. Don't think that I am not aware of the prepared material that is available to retail salespeople in a lot of different businesses. Most people may throw away their junk mail. But I'm in the selling business, so I look at it all. And I think all of us should. But I am strongly recommending the extra work and the extra cost of your own stuff, because it gets through and its selling messages get through. And when you have somebody who remembers you and likes you because of what they get in the mail from you, you have made the best possible investment of your time and your money.

Some of you may be saying, That's great for a car salesman or a real estate salesman but I sell to purchasing agents and they are a different breed of cattle. I still say the mail is a very effective tool (if used right) to get your name in front of a prospect before your competition does. A salesman I know works for a new company in the energy management field. Because the company is small, they cannot afford expensive advertising. This salesman sent out fifty creative pieces of mail, which resulted in a $30,000 sale. Now that's not a bad return on the investment. The dealership where I work was sending out mail long before I started working there—I just found a better way to do it. The secret is in how creative and interesting you can make it. With a little imagination you could think of a dozen things to do with mail. Perhaps you could send useful "how to" tips. You could clip news items out of the paper and send them to your customers with a little note that just says, "Hi John, thought this might interest you. Joe Girard." Some salesmen send expensive personalized calendars. This keeps their name in front of the customer all year long. Another salesman I know keeps postcards in his briefcase and jots off a personal note to his good customers while waiting for an appointment or a plane. Watch the ways in which the giant companies spend millions just to keep their name in front of the public. I have learned from them, and you should too, because we have businesses just like them, only maybe not so big.

That, after all, is what it is about: Your time is limited and your money (whether it is your own or is supplemented by your employer) is limited. So you are making an investment in mailing that will provide you with personal leverage. You can't afford to make cold personal calls at the homes or offices of all your prime prospects. They probably wouldn't like you to appear unannounced anyway. But by making *effective* use of your time and money in planning and executing attractive, personal mailings, you get the next best thing: You get something of yourself into their homes, causing them to remember you, like you, and, at the right time, buy from you. That is the kind of high-quality, personal investment leverage we should try for all the time in the selling profession.

Get your name in front of your prospects whenever you can —and get it into their homes.

11

Hunting with Birddogs

Nobody in this business is so good at it that he can't use help. I'll take all the help I can get, and I'll pay whatever it is worth to get it. I have already given you some idea of how much money I spend on direct mail to my prospect list. Though there are thousands of names on that list, they are my prime prospects. I didn't buy that list. I don't depend on what some commercial mail-order list company thinks are my prospects. I built my own list, name by name. It was a gradual process, so I could always afford what it cost to reach those people. Because the mailings helped to bring them back. And that has earned me more than enough to continue using this method to build business.

But, as I said before, it is an investment. That means that I have to pay my share of the mailing costs up front, before the fruits from the mailings are harvested. But, as I pointed out, I get something else besides valuable goodwill from my mailings. I recruit new birddogs, and I remind the others that I am still here, ready to pay for sales.

Maybe you don't use the term "birddogs," but whatever you call them, they are people who send other people to me to buy cars. And I pay them for those sales—$25 apiece—but not until they are sold. So the money I pay to birddogs—about $14,000 last year—is not an investment. It does not go out up front. It is a cost of sales. But in my tax bracket—and in the bracket of anybody who really devotes himself to being a professional salesman—the $25.00 I pay out for a sale already in the hand costs me only $12.50, because the other $12.50 would have gone to the government as income tax. There are a lot of dealers who pay half of the money due the birddog. My dealer does not pay anything to me or to any other salesman. I pay the entire $25.00—$12.50 from me and $12.50 from Uncle Sam.

I have a very strict rule about paying birddogs. *I pay them.* I don't stall them. I don't try to do them out of the money on some technicality. *I pay them.* Suppose a person sends in somebody with my card and forgets to write his name on the back and the customer does not mention that somebody sent him. After the sale, I'll probably get a call from the person asking, "How come you didn't send me the money when you sold Sterling Jones that Impala?" And I tell him, "I'm sorry. Your name wasn't on the card and Jones didn't say anything to me. So come on by this afternoon and pick up the money. It's waiting for you. But next time put your name on the card, so I can get the money to you quicker."

Keep Your Promise—They'll Love You for It

The point is that when you have told people you will pay them for a sale, you have made them a promise. You have given them your word. If you "stiff" them, you become a liar and a cheat. Try that on 250 people and see what happens. Wait a minute, you say, what if the guy stiffed you? What if he didn't really send Jones in. My answer is that this could happen once in a while. But not very often, because just about everybody who is likely to be a birddog is in my files. And even if somebody did stiff me for $12.50 out of my pocket and another $12.50 out of Uncle Sam's, I still earned a good commission on the sale. And if the guy tells anybody else about it, he is probably going to say what a great guy I am. And that's worth at least $12.50.

But the reason I am such a soft touch is not that I especially like to give away money. It is because the risk of not paying somebody who really earned the money is just too big. When I look at the odds, I figure it is better to pay the birddog fee to 50 guys who didn't earn it than not to pay it to one guy who did earn it. Maybe even 100 to 1.

I told you that I paid out $14,000 to birddogs last year. That means I got about 550 sales, or about one out of every three, from my birddogs. They sent me business that made me roughly $75,000 in commissions. And that business cost me $14,000. That is what I consider a pretty fair exchange, especially when you figure that most of this was extra business that I would not have got at all without paying for it.

Where do I find birddogs? I find them in the same ways that you will. I am going to tell you in detail how I get them and keep them.

Everybody Can Be Your Birddog

The process started for me with the question: Whom do I know that would like to get $25 for sending me a sale? I don't know any Rockefellers, but I know some people who earn pretty big money, and I cannot think of anybody I know who would not be glad to pick up an extra $25 for sending me a customer. I once paid a fee to a brain surgeon whose biggest money problem is storing it. And I have several ministers who send me a lot of $25 business.

When I make a sale and the customer takes delivery of his

car (all this will be discussed in detail in separate chapters), the last thing I do as he drives out is put a stack of my business cards along with the one that explains my birddog arrangement in the glove compartment of the car. A few days later, when he gets my thank-you card, he also gets another stack of cards. He is now a birddog. He is also on my mailing list, so at least once a year he gets a mailing that includes my birddog recruiting kit as a reminder that my offer is still good.

A satisfied customer is obviously an easy source of other business. If my deal was good enough for him, it ought to be good enough for his friends and his relatives, he has to figure. That goes for anybody. But when I find that my customer is somebody who is a leader, somebody that other people listen to, I make an extra effort to make him a good deal and to recruit him as a birddog.

If I meet somebody who is a shop steward or a local union president, I know I am talking to somebody who has a lot of influence over other union officials as well as his membership. He is somebody who is political. He talks to a lot of people, and he wants them to like him so they'll vote for him. In a way, he is in the same situation that I'm in and that you're in. He is a kind of salesman in his own field, selling himself, which is after all what we have to do, no matter how good our products and our prices are.

So when I run into anybody like that, I recognize that he is worth a lot of effort because, if I treat him well, he will work very hard for me. If he gets a good deal from me, he will work hard for me, because he will be working hard for himself. He will be trying to give his supporters a good deal, so he will send them to me so that I can do for them what I did for him. If you work something like that properly, you get fantastic leverage from it. It is like extending yourself in hundreds of different directions.

Sometimes people won't take money from me for sending me sales. It bothers them for lots of reasons. In some cases, they really are grateful to me for giving them a good deal on their own car, so they think I've done enough for them and they're glad to send other people to me. A few of those people even return the $25 check when I send it to them. If they do, I call them and apologize for whatever is bothering them. But that doesn't happen too often, you can bet, because $25 is $25.

There are some problems with paying people cash. In some places, it is against the law. I am not a lawyer, so I don't know the full extent of those laws. But I do know that in a lot of places you can give people gifts or free services where you can't give them cash. I don't want to be recommending anything that could cause you to break the law. So if you want to have effective birddogs and you can't pay cash, you had better find out for yourself what you can do legally in the area where you do business.

What is necessary in developing a big and effective system of birddogs is to make it worth their while. I have found that $25 or its equivalent is the minimum amount that will work on most people. Less than that, and there will only be a trickle of extra business. But I don't want people to feel guilty about getting paid for doing me a favor. I want them to feel rewarded and I want them to feel obligated, but I don't want them to feel guilty. Mostly they don't, though, so it is not a big problem.

How to Pay If They Won't Take Cash

When people tell me that they don't want to be paid cash for sending me sales, I handle it in a different way. If somebody is sent in by a birddog, I make it a practice to phone the birddog and thank him and tell him that I am putting his $25 check in the mail. If he says he is not allowed to accept money because of some employer rule or for any other reason, I tell him that I would like to do something else nice for him. Then I contact a good restaurant in Detroit where I know the management. I ask them to send my birddog a card entitling him and his wife to be my guest for dinner. Or if he is not the sort who would like that, I may send him a note telling him that he can bring his car into our place for a certain amount of free service.

I offer these ideas to you as ways of getting around whatever legal or other problems you may have in your area that would stop you from paying cash for your birddog business. Mostly, though, I have found that if I send somebody a check at his home address, there is no problem.

Now I realize that in some fields it's not ethical to reward a birddog financially, but that's no reason to not use them. Sales managers are constantly telling me that if they could only get their salesmen to ask for referrals they would be making more money. Let's talk about that. When you ask a customer for a referral you're actually doing him a favor. Here's how. Most people like to help others; they enjoy passing along a good tip about a great deal or a nice salesman. If you treated them right they'll be happy to tell their friends about you. If the friend also buys, it gives the original customer a good feeling that he was able to help a friend. Also, almost everyone feels a need to toot his own horn now and then. Bragging about what a good deal they got fills that need. When a friend buys on their recommendation it reinforces their belief in their own good judgment. Let's face it, you and I do the same thing for the people we like—our doctor, dentist, barber and painter. So why hesitate to ask others to help you build your business? You both benefit.

Get Your Barber to Talk About You

One of my favorite sources of birddogs is barbers. They do a lot of talking to their customers—too much, some people think. Anyway, I try to get a haircut at a different barbershop in my area every time I need one. Thus, I can circulate among a lot of barbers and recruit them and bolster their interest.

The way I usually begin with a barber is to bring him a small sign that I have prepared for me by a local commercial art studio. It is an easel card and it says: ASK ME ABOUT THE BEST CAR DEAL IN TOWN. I offer that sign to the barber, explain my $25 payment, and leave him a stack of my cards. Notice that the sign does not mention Chevrolet. In fact, I tell the barber to ask other customers who are salesmen of other makes of cars if they will make the same $25 payments that I offer. I tell him to get their cards too. That way, when somebody notices the sign and asks him about it, he can ask them what kind of car they want. If they say a Buick, he has a card from the Buick salesman. Or Volkswagen or Ford or whatever. I have put him into a business that will make him a lot of extra money if he works it. And I get my share, or more than my share, of that business.

As I said, I have done that with many barbers. I also do it with just about anybody I run into. I don't mean I give out signs to everybody. So far I have only used them with barbers. But you would be surprised who will work for you for that $25.

For instance, there is a major manufacturer of pharmaceuticals in this area, and that company employs a lot of doctors. I have several doctors at that company among my birddogs, and they are among the most productive on my entire list. They make good money on their jobs, they work with other people who make good money, they talk to a lot of other doctors and people on hospital staffs, and often these people own several cars. Not only that, but they go to a lot of meetings and conventions where they run into other doctors and people in their industry. It is a big and wealthy industry, and this, plus the fact that doctors seem to be at least as eager for money as anybody else, brings me a lot of extra business.

Among the most important ways I get birddogs is through banks, finance companies, and credit unions. I am talking about the people who approve the loans that many people have to get to buy new cars. These loan people are not very well paid. In fact, they get paid lousy for being in the money business and handing out a lot of money to other people. So they are glad to earn extra from me—at $25 a head.

I go after them. Sometimes I will pick the name off the check or the loan approval that a customer brings in when he is buying a car. After the sale, I'll phone the man at the bank or loan office and tell him that I am the guy who just sold Al Robinson that Monte Carlo, and that it was nice doing business with him and his organization. What I want to do then is take him out to lunch. It doesn't matter where in the area he is located. I'll tell him I just happen to be going to that neighborhood that day, and we arrange to meet at the best restaurant we can think of around there. Why not? What if it costs me $25 or even $50 for lunch? It's a business expense, and besides, if I get one extra sale from that lunch, I've made good money on it.

When I meet him at the restaurant, I tell him over lunch what it's all about. I mention that I'll pay a reward of $25 for every customer who buys from me who brings in a card with his name on the back. Or else maybe he'll just want to phone me and mention that he is sending somebody over. I tell him how big my volume is so that he will understand that I have a lot of satisfied customers. He will also get the message that I can usually beat anybody else's deal. This often gets me a chance to bid against a deal from another salesman.

Let me explain: Suppose that a customer comes into the bank with an order for a car he wants to buy from another dealer. He asks for a loan. The loan officer, who is a birddog of mine, will look at the total price of the deal, excuse himself and go into the next room to phone me. He will tell me what kind of car the man is buying, what optional equipment is on it, and what the price is. I do some quick figuring to see what I can do to beat the price. I try to come up with a figure that is about $50 lower than what the man has got from the place he went to buy the other car.

O.K., now suppose that I can come up with a price that is $50 lower. I give it to the loan officer and let him know that I have the car and can do business right away. He goes back to his office and tells the customer that I can give him the same car at a price that is $50 lower. If the price is only $25 lower, the customer may not think it is worth coming to me. After all, he may have left a deposit—say, $10 or $20—with the other salesman. For $50 less, he can afford to lose that deposit. Anything less, he may figure it is not worth the trouble to come over and see me. Also, the loan officer is going to get $25 for sending me the deal, so he will encourage the customer as much as he can, telling him what a reliable dealership and salesman and all that.

As soon as I have finished talking to the loan officer, I find a car in our inventory as near as possible to the one the guy wanted, exactly the same if we have it or if I can get it quickly from another dealer. I have the shop wash it and get it ready for delivery. I know that when the customer comes in, he is going to have his credit approved for the amount he needs to own the car.

What I have done by making that loan officer a birddog is to put him in a position where he can send me business I could not possibly have got in any other way. He got me a sale that was already sold by another salesman. He helped his loan customer by saving him money, he earned $25 for himself, and he got me a sale I had no way of getting. Even with the birddog fee and the price cut I gave the customer, I am still going to earn some commission. Even if I net only $50 for myself on that sale, that is still $50 I could not have got in any other way.

That was found money, right from the sky into my pocket. Think about that. Think about how I created that extra money for myself. And think about how you can do things like that in your business.

Here are some other ways and places that I find people to

work for me as birddogs. Whenever I buy gas and oil, I try to talk to people around the station, especially if it does repair work too. They see a lot of cars that need to be replaced. When a guy comes in with a car that needs extensive repair work—say, $500 or so—he is not very far from starting to think about buying a new car instead of fixing the old one. If he says he will hold off on having the car fixed, he is already probably beginning to think about buying a new one. It may take only a word or two from the man at the repair garage to plant the idea of coming to see me with one of my cards in his hand. If the customer isn't going to have the work done right away, the mechanic isn't out anything if he birddogs him to me, and he may make himself $25 which he wouldn't be getting otherwise.

Among the best sources of birddog business are towing services and body bump shops. They see a lot of cars that have been totaled and that aren't going to be repaired. The owner is going to have to buy a new car, and chances are he is going to be getting a check from an insurance company. People who work in accident insurance claims and sales offices are also good choices as birddogs, because they too know about wrecked cars. I try to make contact with all of these people, because they are excellent sources of business for me.

Birddogging Your Birddogs

But once you have made contact and have passed the word about the fee you pay and left them with your cards, you still have to keep in touch. When things are slow and I have some spare time, I am likely to go through my birddog file just to see who has not been sending me any business. Then I will call up and shoot the breeze and ask how come I haven't been sending them any $25 checks lately. They may just have forgotten. If they were new birddogs, they may not have got into the habit of suggesting buying a new car from me.

Some of my birddogs send me a steady stream of prospects, because they sense opportunities whenever they arise. Others need to be prodded at the beginning of the relationship, and even long afterward. It is a matter of how easy or how hard it is for other people to develop the habit of reacting at the right moment to earn that extra $25 from me. Everybody has to develop new habits. It took me a while to develop the sense of who can produce extra business for me.

I keep finding people all the time, because I have learned to look for people all the time, wherever I am. I go to my health club to work out after business hours, and I make sure that the locker room attendant and the masseur know what I do and have some of my cards. I don't make a big thing out of it, and I get business from other members without birddogs. But you always have to watch for opportunities, and sometimes there are certain kinds that you might not expect in advance.

Consider this one: I get a phone call one afternoon from a fellow who wants a price on a certain car. There are probably as many ways to handle such phone calls as there are salesmen. I usually take the call and give a price on the phone. Some salesmen will give a price so low that the caller will have to come in, even though the salesman can't possibly deliver a car at the price. We call that "copping a plea." Some salesmen call it "low-balling." All it is intended to do is keep the customer from shopping somewhere else. Then what happens is that he comes in and the salesman tries to switch him to a different model or other options or else, if he has to, he says that the sales manager wouldn't approve the price and squeezes some more money out of him.

I don't approve of that practice and neither do other legitimate salesmen. It is bad business because the customer feels cheated even if he buys from you. And if he doesn't, he writes you off as some kind of crook. That means at least 250 people are going to be told that you are a wrong guy.

When I get a phone call, I give the caller a legitimate price.

We'll talk about the range of prices in this business in another chapter. But right now just take my word for it that a salesman has a very wide range of prices that he can quote to a prospect, because there are dozens of models, many kinds of options, and other factors that create hundreds, even thousands of combinations, all at different prices.

Obviously, when I get that kind of phone call, I want to give the caller a price that will bring him in. If he doesn't mention air conditioning, mag wheels, and an AM-FM pushbutton stereo cassette and CB combination radio, I don't quote him a price with all those things on the car. I don't even want to talk to him about extras, because I want to quote a price that is low yet legitimate for a car I actually can deliver.

I also want to talk to the man long enough to find out if he has been shopping around, and also to learn what he does for a living so I will know if arranging credit for him will be easy or hard. I also want to know how much it would be worth to me and to my dealer to sell this customer, even at a very low profit margin, even at a loss.

A Freebie That Works for You

That's right: I may be willing to give up all of my commission on a sale and even reimburse my dealer if it looks like the prospect is worth selling at less than cost. Let's consider this caller. He tells me exactly what he wants on his car. I find out that he has shopped at other dealers, and he gives me the lowest price he has been quoted. It turns out that he has a price that I can beat only by losing money out of my pocket.

I have an arrangement with my dealer to the effect that if somebody is really important for us to sell at a loss, I can do it if I get permission first and then make up out of my own pocket anything less than dealer cost that I want to sell the car for. Now that is not a situation I want to be in very often. I like

to make money as well as friends when I sell cars. But sometimes a customer can be so important that he is worth the loss
to me, and the dealer is willing to let a car go for no immediate profit to him. At least he gets his money out of it and
reduces his inventory. But he also has to see a reason for no
profit right away.

In a typical case—and there are not too many of them
—the caller turned out to be a unit chairman of his union in
a big Chevrolet parts plant. That meant that he had a lot of
influence over a lot of people who own cars and mostly buy
Chevrolets for a lot of obvious reasons, including the fact that
sometimes cars of one manufacturer are not treated well in the
parking lots of factories where cars of other manufacturers are
made. That is not nice, but it is how it is sometimes in this
business. So this fellow calls up with this very low price
already in hand. I tell him what a good price he has, and he
knows it. Then I tell him to hold on, and I check with the
manager about quoting a price at a loss. I get the O.K., and
I give the customer a price $50 below dealer cost. When he
hears the price, he knows I have beaten every other deal,
because he knows the numbers and may know I am going to
lose on the deal. So he comes in and, assuming that I can't
sell him on any extras that might raise the price and especially
the profit margin a little, he gets delivery on the car at the
price I quoted, and I have to give the dealer $50 of my money.

What happens now? I have developed, at a cost of $50
(not counting the commission I didn't earn on the sale), a
birddog who will brag about the deal he got and tout me and
my dealer all over his union and his plant and his neighborhood. He'll talk about me to the boys in his bowling league,
at the marina where he keeps his boat, and everywhere else
he goes.

Of course, when he left with his new car, he also got a stack
of my business cards and a pitch about how I pay $25 for
every sale he sends me. But even without that he would send

me and the dealership a lot of business, enough to more than make up for the money we lost on him.

Since many people tend to brag about how cheap they buy their cars, those who hear him probably won't expect to buy as cheap as he did. And let me assure you that none of them will. My dealer is entitled to a fair profit and I am entitled to a fair commission. We are not in business to give away merchandise. But sometimes that's the very best way to build volume and profit.

If I get only one regular sale from that customer, I have more than made back the loss from selling him. And so has my dealer. But I may see a dozen or more people come in as a result of that one $50 seed that I planted. And remember that the $50 is a business expense that I charge off when I figure my taxes, so it costs me $25 out of pocket.

A lot of times you will be approached by police and sheriffs and firemen to buy tickets to their social functions. Even the mailmen have them in some places. I am sure that you have the sense not to turn down people like that for a lot of reasons, especially if you are in business. But I have found that they make first-rate birddogs. So when I get the chance, I'll buy their tickets and then offer them a stack of my cards and tell them about my $25 policy. The same works for fraternal organizations. When their people come around selling ads in the program books of their affairs, I always buy an ad. But I don't go for those that read: COMPLIMENTS OF A FRIEND. Mine always say something like: BEST WISHES FROM JOE GIRARD, MEROLLIS CHEVROLET. I send a stack of cards to the person who solicited the ad. And if I have the time, I go to their functions, because they are good places to meet people and let them know what I do for a living. I know that a lot of other people, including dentists and insurance salesmen, do the same thing. But that only proves that it is a good way to build your business.

Anybody who talks to other people every day in his work

can be a birddog. And keep in mind especially those people who traditionally don't make much money, like the loan officers at banks. Not only don't they get paid much, but they hardly ever get taken to lunch or get gifts of any kind in their business life. That's why I always look to take people like that to lunch. They remember it well. It is a big deal to them if you take them to a place they really can't afford to go to, and you spend 10 or 12 deductible dollars on them. And I also do something else for them. Before I go to meet them, I put a half-gallon bottle of Crown Royal whisky in the back of my car. It happens to be considered one of the top brands in these parts. And after they get out of the car and we are saying goodbye, I reach in back, hold it up, and say, "Listen, Harry, somebody gave me this bottle and I don't drink much Canadian whisky, so I was wondering if you wouldn't mind taking it, please." You bet he allows me to persuade him to take it, and every time he pours a drink from that big bottle, he remembers my name and what I do for a living and what I can do for him.

I have heard other salesmen complain sometimes about birddogs when they first start to use them. One fellow said to me, "I started giving out cards a month ago, and I haven't got a single sale from any of them." My answer is always the same: *Just be patient. You've planted the seeds. Just keep on planting. There will be plenty to harvest.* Last year, as I said, I sold about 550 cars through birddogs. A lot of salesmen would have been happy to have that as their total sales for the year. And I don't know how many customers I sold through word of mouth that started with cards I passed out to birddogs. The chain is endless if you keep it going. And the cost is almost nothing, because it is all extra business.

Paying $25 can make you hundreds, but you really have to pay it to get that payoff.

12

Knowing What You're Doing— and Why

One of the corniest slogans in sales training, you used to hear it all the time and maybe you still do, is this one: *Plan your work and work your plan.* I've heard it a hundred times at least. And I am sure that everybody above a certain age in the automobile selling business has heard it that much or more. It used to be said so often everybody made jokes about it.

But let me tell you something that I have learned in my years in this business. That is the best advice you can get. The trouble with the slogan is that it is so cute and tricky, and it is said so much it loses its meaning. But what it means is still the best advice you can get. It really says two different things. One is that you should be in command of yourself and of what you do. This means that you are not operating by a series of accidents, such as who happens to walk through the door of your place of business when you are at the head of the line of salesmen. Two is that if you figure out the right moves to make and make them, they will bring in business for you.

I have talked about business cards and direct mail and birddogs and phone calls. I have not said very much about what we mostly think of as selling. I have said very little about what you say to the prospect when you finally have him face-to-face. I will say a good bit about that in the chapters to come. But if you don't read beyond this chapter and if you do the things I have described, you will sell a lot of whatever it is that you sell. That will happen for several reasons, but the most important of those reasons is that you will get a lot of people coming in and asking for you or you'll have more prospects to call on. And even if you are only an average or below-average presenter and closer, you are bound to do a lot better than you ever did before in your life.

You Don't Have to Close Better to Sell More

Remember that we have been talking about planting and harvesting, filling and emptying the seats on the Ferris wheel. We have been talking about the odds and the probabilities of business. Now there is no way you can doubt that if you do everything in the face-to-face selling situation exactly the way you have always done it before, you will sell a lot more if you do it a lot more. We are now talking about nothing but quantity.

I am deadly serious. If you get twice as many people to come to you every day, you will sell twice as many people as you used to. If your normal pace is to sell 50 percent of your customers, and you have two a day, you get one sale a day. That is basic arithmetic. You don't have to have a high school diploma to figure that out. But now let's go to some bigger numbers. If you manage to get four customers a day and do the same thing as before, you will still sell only half of them. But now you will be getting two sales a day. You have just doubled your output.

You think I am trying to be funny, but I'm not. I am deadly

serious, as I said before. Just stop and think how much time you spend doing nothing but waiting for traffic through the door or a lead to call in. Up to now, maybe you thought that was how it works. Maybe you figured that what you were making was all that you could expect to make unless you got lucky. You have probably had hot streaks when everything worked for you, the traffic streamed through the door, and everybody who came in bought twice what they usually buy. Wow! you said. If only I could keep this up!

Well, let me tell you something: You can keep it up. For sure, you can get more people to come in to see you. And even if they only buy as often and as much as before, you will be on a permanent hot streak compared to your usual volume. How to boost your "kill rate" is another story, and we'll get to some parts of it.

But that really doesn't matter at all if you get the first part right; that is, if you get more people coming through the door to see you. And the way you do that is to go back to that tired old slogan—plan your work and work your plan—and do it. Do it. Do it!

Work Smart—Not Hard

I am not joking. What I am saying is that the way to get the job done is to decide what it is—every day. I mean you must—I don't say should—take some time every morning and decide what you are going to do that day. And then you must do it. Don't get me wrong. I am not sitting here preaching about the glories of hard work. I don't believe in hard work. I believe in good work. I believe in smart work. I believe in effective work—work that works.

So what I do every morning is figure out what I am going to do that day. The first thing I do is check my appointment book to see what I am locked into. It might be a lunch with a finance company loan officer. It might be that I called some customer the other day who was due for a new car. It is a good thing to arrange your card file of sold customers in more than one way. You want to have them alphabetically so you can find somebody by name. But it also helps to have another set by date, so that if somebody bought from you yesterday he goes to the back of that file, and so on. That way you can start from the front and see who is due. Sometimes when I have some free time, I call those people just to remind them that maybe they want to come in and talk about a new car. I will do that with a lot of the list around the time the new models come in. If I have been doing that lately, I will have a number of appointments in my book, spread over a month or so. That is because I try to get people to set a day and time when they will be in. I don't just say, "Sam, the new cars are in and I hope you drop by to see them." I lay it on them: "Come on in this afternoon, Sam, about four, O.K.?" If he can't make it then, he has to give me a time when he can, and then I have a customer coming in. And I write it down in my book then and there. I have a pretty good memory, but I never trust it.

All right, so I check my book and see that I have an appointment in the afternoon. Obviously, I can't predict who will come in out of the blue and ask for me. A lot of people do every day. I am not surprised when they do, because practically everything I do every day is aimed at getting that flow of people in to me. But there will be free time during every day, and I want to be sure that I am going to be filling it with something designed to get even more of them in.

Since my direct mail program is too big for me to handle on my own these days, I have people who do the work for me. But in the days before it reached its present scale, I did it myself, sending out a certain number of pieces every morning. Usually I did it during the times when I was next up and had nothing else to do. At those times, I wanted to be able to leave whatever I was doing to handle the next customer through the door, because it was my turn. Addressing mail is the safest thing to be doing at those times. If you're on the phone when you're up, you run the risk of having to tell a live phone prospect that you'll call him back. And that is something you never want to do.

But when I was not up, I would be working on some direct mail or making some calls. Or I would be building some good-will somewhere on the premises, maybe out back in the service department. (I'll explain later how important I consider my relations with that part of the operation.) Or maybe I am upstairs talking to the people on the office staff. The administrative part of a sales operation can make the difference between a satisfied and a dissatisfied customer, even when *you* do everything right.

Lose One Day—But Not 250

But I want to say one thing about my work schedule. If I get up in the morning and feel depressed for some reason and I can't shake it, I may decide not to go to work at all. Or I may look out the window and decide it's a good day to go out in my boat. I don't do that very often, maybe once or twice a year. And I don't recommend *not* working as a way to build business. But sometimes you know you just aren't going to be worth anything on the job. If you go in on that day, you may wind up making a bad mistake or getting into a fight with somebody that will cost you 250 people.

If that seems like what the day is going to be about, you are better off not going in. Cancel your appointments if you have any, and then play golf or go to a movie or to the races or treat yourself well in some other way. That's not to say that you are not treating yourself well when you work well and make money and please customers. But if you really are convinced that you won't do anybody any good by going to work for a morning or an afternoon or a whole day, then don't do it. Because you don't want to carry dissatisfactions of any kind into your place of business. They can be like a contagious disease.

If those feelings keep up for more than a day, you've got problems that I can't help you solve. But if they happen just once in a while, then plan your day to do something else. But be damned sure that the reason you are feeling dissatisfied isn't because you didn't do a good job the day before. Because if that's why you feel that way, I have found that the best way to cure it is to go in to work with a plan and a resolve to do better.

One sure way to get over the dissatisfactions of a bad day is to review that day and try to understand why what happened to you happened. I do that at the end of *every* working day. I replay the day, examining every sale I made and every one I lost. That's right. I don't sell everybody I see. Which is why I spend so much of my money and energy making sure that I will see a lot of people. I play the percentages I recommend that you play. Maybe I sell only half the people I see in a day. But that usually means I see at least ten people and sell at least five of them. I have been averaging better than five cars a day every day in recent years, not because I have a high kill rate but because I have a high prospect rate.

But I go over every contact I made during the day. What did I say to that fellow that finally made him buy? Why did that other guy from East Detroit really not buy? Was he just shopping for sport? Or is that too easy a way to explain away some mistake I made?

When I first began to do this kind of customer-by-customer analysis of my day, if I couldn't think of a mistake I made, I would sometimes call up the customer I lost. I would tell him who I was and why I was calling. People usually want to help you. I'd say I was trying to learn the business and learn from my mistakes. A lot of times they would say that they were Ford or Plymouth guys from way back, but they just wanted to see if Chevrolet maybe had something they ought to know about. That might mean that I didn't sell my product well enough against the competition. Or they might tell me that they got a better price somewhere else. I'd question them very carefully about the optional equipment they got and the trade-in allowance on their car. Sometimes a salesman who has some control over the price he charges gets too greedy and doesn't recognize that a small cut or something extra thrown in can lock up a deal.

Incidentally, my replay of each day is not just my idea. Some of the greatest and most successful people in history developed this habit and attribute much of their success to it. I know that for the time it takes me I have been rewarded handsomely. Want some good advice? Try it.

I always try to compare my own feelings about a customer —especially if I lose him—with what he says about why he didn't buy from me and did buy from somebody else. People sometimes think they know more about themselves and their feelings and reactions than they actually do. And there is nothing more important to learn about yourself than the difference between the way *you* see something and the way the guy on the other side of the deal sees it.

Because you never want to be on the other side. Your success in winning the war comes with narrowing and finally eliminating the gap between you and the customer. You want both of you on the same side, and what this means is that *you* have to do the maneuvering to get you both on the same side, whatever tools and methods you use to do it.

Knowing What You Lost Helps You Win

But I always want to know why I lost every sale I lost. And I hardly ever accept "I was just looking" as the answer, because if somebody takes my time and his to come all the way over to our place just to look, he is already partly sold. And I want to know why I didn't get him totally sold.

I think that this is a rule that is good maybe 95 percent of the time in automobile selling. And it is probably good most of the time in every kind of selling: If someone comes in and is "just looking," he has enough interest to be sold most of the time. So if you let him "just look" every time, you are probably not getting nearly your share of sales. And if you try and fail, don't charge it off in your mind to "just looking." Analyze your performance in the confrontation and try to see where you failed to convert him. Because chances are you did fail.

This sounds like negative rather than positive thinking. But it isn't at all. Look at it this way: You are thinking most positively when you believe that you should be able to sell everybody who comes in. Realistically, of course, nobody can do that. But it is still a very effective attitude to have. It encourages you to analyze every lost sale to see why you lost it so that you can try to correct the mistake next time you run into the same kind of situation.

Just keep in mind that somebody who is "just looking" may really be saying that he is scared of you and of your ability to get him to part with his money—even if it is for something he really wants to buy. I have called the selling situation a war and a contest and a confrontation. But I don't mean that you should act this way when you are in this situation. A wrestling match won't get your customer over his fear. But once you have him in front of you, your most effective approach may be "let him"—not "make him." And that applies to what he wants to look at or talk about or anything else. Because if he feels free—even to walk out—he will get over that first fear, and that's what you want.

I've heard it said that anyone who sells as many cars as I do must be strictly a high-pressure salesman. To me a high-pressure salesman tries to make people buy. I *let* them buy. I believe one of the most important determining factors of a sale is, Does the prospect like, trust and believe me. If I fail to develop these attitudes in a prospect, chances are I've also failed to make a sale. It's pretty tough to make someone like you, but you can, by the things you say and do, let him like you. I feel this philosophy has helped make me number 1, and if you want to make a lot of money selling then you, too, should develop the philosophy, *Let him,* don't make him.

Attitude planning is as much a part of planning your selling day as anything else. If you feel lousy, you still usually have to go to work. So what you have to do is get hold of your negative feeling, whatever it is, and face it, even if you can't make it go away. That way, when you get somebody through the door or on the phone, you can shove your lousy feeling aside. But first you have to recognize how you feel, or else you won't be able to plan and deal with your own feeling. And you can be sure that if you are *not* in control of what is going on inside of you, you will certainly communicate your bad feeling to somebody who comes in suspicious of you to begin with.

When I replay my day each night, I find that I really can have total recall of what I said and did. And I don't fall asleep until I am sure that there was nothing I could have done to convert the "be-backs" and the other lost sales. And remember that the be-back had better be written off the minute he walks out the door. I think I am pretty good at judging customers and hanging onto them. But when I hear a guy say he'll be back, I figure he is gone forever. Sometimes they do come back, because some people really do tell the truth. But if you are counting on be-backs as part of your future earnings, you are still an amateur who is fooling himself.

One thing that I have found—it is something nobody likes to admit—is that maybe somebody else can sell a person if you can't. A lot of businesses require that a salesman turn over a customer to somebody else in the place before they let him walk. I like to think that nobody is better than I am. But nobody is perfect, so it is sometimes useful to bring over somebody else in a way that doesn't make the customer more resistant. You don't want him to think he is being pressured.

For a while, I used to have an arrangement with other salesmen in my place that if they couldn't sell somebody, I would pay them $10 for a chance to try to sell him myself. I won't ask you to believe that I could sell them all. But I did sell some of them. I quit doing that, though, because the other salesmen got sore when I got the big commission and all they got was a $10 bill. They did not accept the idea that my $10 had bought all rights to a customer they had given up on. They wanted to split the commission with me. So I dropped the idea. I suggest that if you want to try anything like that, you make sure that everybody understands—in advance—the terms of the arrangement. But I also recommend trying it sometime, because there is no better practice of your selling techniques than working on somebody who is about to walk out. And there is no better feeling than when you convert one into a sale.

In a way, it is one of the very best tests of your skills. But if you are going to try it, be sure that you know something about the selling methods and techniques of the other people in your place of business. That way you can try something different from what the other salesman did. There is no point in doing and saying the same things to the customer that the other salesman tried. You want to approach him differently. Of course, sometimes it is useful to do it straight on by asking him what he was looking for or needed that the other fellow didn't show him. You don't want to run down the people you work with. But sometimes if you ask a question like that, it will let a person know that you are trying to help him, and he will let down his guard and help sell himself.

As I have been saying, the most important thing a salesman can do is get them through the door so he can face them. Getting them in requires planning. And planning requires making a lot of decisions about who your best prospects are and how they can be reached most efficiently and economically. You have to make decisions about the cost of getting a prospect and his potential value once you get him. But what

determines cost and value is the availability of your time. If
you have a lot of unoccupied time and you work well on the
telephone, it may be most economical some days to concentrate on phoning old customers or even be-backs, if you were
able to get their names and addresses before they got away.

Phone calls may work well for you, but they take a lot of
time per call and per prospect. When you don't have that kind
of time, sending out a few mailing pieces is as good as any
other way of using free time. It certainly is the most useful way
to fill up time when you are next up on the floor, because you
can interrupt any time your next customer walks in. The point
is that you can plan this kind of activity with a lot of accuracy.
The unexpected happens almost every day to most salesmen,
so you can't nail everything down perfectly. And you should
be ready to change your plan whenever something clearly
more productive comes along.

The value of the plan for keeping yourself moving and
keeping the flow of prospects coming in is obvious. But even
when you have to change plans, you still get a lot of mo-
mentum by having a plan in the first place. If I know exactly
what I intend to do when I come into the showroom in the
morning, that knowing motivates me a lot more strongly than
an attitude of wait-and-see.

You've probably been told all kinds of things to say to yourself in the mirror to lift your spirits and clear your mind of
negative thoughts. I certainly don't want to knock any of that
if it works for you. But in my own experience, I don't know
anything that gets me closer to that first sale of the day than
the plan I make every morning. Because when I walk out the
door of my house in the morning, one thing is for sure: I know
where I'm going and what I'm going to do. And whether or
not the whole thing changes the minute I walk into the office
doesn't matter. Because I came in with motivation, with
assurance that I had an important reason for being there. And
that is a most important reason for planning your work—even

if you can't work out every (or any) detail of your plan that day.

It is the first push that you give yourself that moves you closest to the first sale. And I don't have to tell a professional salesman how important the first sale of the day is. You know how good it feels. You know it makes you feel that you are in the right business at the right place at the right time.

Plan your work every day, and work your plan if you can. That may be an old-time, old-fashioned slogan. But I think I have demonstrated how much value it still has for all of us. And then finish your day with a review of everything you did to see how good your plan was and how realistic it was. If you keep falling short of all you intended to do, don't beat yourself up. Maybe your problem is that you are trying to do too much. I'm not trying to let anybody off the hook. All of us work pretty hard a lot of the time. But the question, as I have said, isn't how *hard* we work but how *well*. So if you planned to make ten phone calls and made only five, did you work your plan for those five? That is the kind of thing you want to ask yourself when you review your day.

This is the kind of question that really gives you the measure of your motivation and of your effectiveness as a professional.

Plan your work. Work your plan. Do it!

13

Honesty Is the Best Policy

When I say that honesty is the best policy, I mean exactly that: It's a policy and the best one you can follow most of the time. But a policy, as I mean it, is not a law or a rule. It is something that you use in your work when it is in your best interests. Telling the truth usually is in your best interests, of course, especially if it is about something that a customer can check up on later. Nobody in his right mind would dream of telling a customer he had bought an eight-cylinder car when what you sold him was a six-cylinder model. The first time he opened the hood and counted the wires coming out of the distributor cap, you would be dead, because he would bad-mouth you to a lot more than 250 people.

That's not the kind of thing I am talking about when I suggest that maybe there are times when you won't tell the truth to a prospect. Suppose a prospect calls me up and asks me if I have a certain car, equipped a certain way. Do you know what I am going to tell him? That's right. I am going to say, "I have one out on the lot and you can pick it up today." Now I may have been telling the truth or I may not, because I do not look at the inventory file when I get a call like that. I want the man to come in. Chances are I do have the car, because we carry a very large inventory. Or if I don't, I can get it very fast, because we have an arrangement with other dealers in this area where we trade cars with them, so that we all sort of operate out of the same areawide pool. But what if I have everything he wants except a pushbutton radio? Or maybe I even have a car with exactly the right radio—or can get it—but I have it in gray instead of powder blue. How much of a lie am I telling the customer? A very small one at most. And anyway, when he comes in, if he complains, I can blame it on a mistake in the records.

Most people who want to buy a car want to buy it now. And that's when I want to sell it. It might take a month to special-order the exact one he wants. And in most cases a person is not that hung up on every last detail of the automobile he has set his mind on. There are a couple of dozen or so colors, and the factory would not be painting the cars in all those colors if a lot of people didn't like them. So I am giving him pretty much what he wants. When you ask the butcher for a pound of sirloin, you don't tell him to "stuff" it if it is 15 or 17 ounces instead of 16 ounces, just as long as you don't have to pay for what you're not getting.

I am not recommending that anybody lie to anybody. I really do believe that honesty is the best policy. But honesty is a matter of degree. It is never all one way or the other.

When a customer comes in with his wife and son, and you say, "That's a handsome little boy you have there," is that true or false? He may be the most miserable looking kid in history. But you sure aren't going to say that, if you are looking to make some money. If you are selling a man a new overcoat, you're going to look at his old one and say, "You sure got good wear out of that one," even if what you are thinking is, *That went out of style two years before you bought it and you should have thrown it away before it got threadbare in the elbows.*

He'll Like What You're Selling If You Like What He Has

All of this probably sounds obvious to you, but I have seen salesmen kill a deal by trying to put down the customer with the truth rather than tell a small, kind lie. When a customer asks the salesman how much he'll allow for his trade-in, I have heard salesmen say, "That piece of junk!" Now the car may have four bald tires and no spare. It may be burning more oil than a diesel engine. It may smell like the locker room after a basketball game. But it is his. And it got him to you. And he may love it. Even if he doesn't, it's up to him to knock it. If you do, you are insulting the man. So lie a little. Tell him how good a driver he must have been to get 120,000 miles out of any car. That will make him feel good, so good in fact that he may not give you much argument when you offer him only what it is really worth.

What I am getting at is not just that people like to be flattered even when they know that what you're saying isn't completely true. More important, it creates a pleasant, disarming atmosphere when you toss off a few small compliments about his wife's dress, his kid's cuteness, or even the eyeglass frames he is wearing.

Whatever you say like that, it is small talk that gets the customer over those first fears that you want to take the gold out of his teeth. It is what military men call a diversionary action. And even if the guy doesn't respond, I try to keep it up until I get him to give a little. I'll get into other kinds of conversational topics later. But you never want to get so involved with some other subject that you forget why he came in. He may, but you never should, not even for a second.

You are an actor in the selling situation, and that is something you never should forget. Timing is the most valuable quality any performer can have. But it is something you have to work into. When I want to get away for a weekend, I usually go to Las Vegas. I do it for a couple of reasons. One, because that is the only place I gamble. I don't expect to win, but I never bet so much that I can't afford to lose. I know what the odds are, and I know that they are against me. But it's fun.

The second reason I go to Las Vegas is to watch one of the best performers in the world, Don Rickles. I watch his timing, his facial expressions, even the way he does his famous insults. Not that I ever want to insult a customer, but I want to watch the way he can dump on somebody in the audience and then turn the person's anger into a smile. Turning anger into a smile is like what we do: turning fear into trust. Turning no into yes.

You want the customer to trust you while you are selling him, and you want him to trust you after he leaves. That is why you never want to tell him a big lie that he can check later. You never want to tell him anything that he will get laughed at by his friends and relatives for believing. You never want to tell him anything that will make him feel foolish later. And sometimes you want to stop a person from doing something on his own that will embarrass him later.

There are a lot of businesses where the real price of a product varies a lot from what is on the price tag. In the car business, as everybody knows, there is a sticker on the window of every new car with the manufacturer's suggested price at the bottom of that sticker. Most people know that most cars can be bought for less than what it says on the sticker. Some, like Corvettes, are hard to get and do sell for the sticker price. So did Cadillac convertibles and a lot of imported cars. But most American cars can be bought for less than that price tag and, as I said, most people know that.

But some people don't, especially if they come from a rural

town where the one or two dealers don't give the usual discounts. Sometimes somebody will come in to me, look at a car, and start to write a check for the full amount on the window sticker. What's wrong with that? you ask. Nothing, really. That's what it says on the price tag, and a lot of people expect to pay the price and don't even know how to haggle. Some people just don't like to do that.

Then why not take the customer's money? Well, in a lot of businesses, that's what you do. But in the car business, especially selling a high-volume car like Chevrolet that you can buy anywhere, this can be risky. A lot of car salesmen don't agree with me. But I think they are wrong to take the full price every time somebody really wants to pay it. Suppose that the customer buys the car and goes to his lodge meeting. One of the things about new cars is that people love to show them off to their friends and neighbors. That can be a very effective way to close a deal, as I will describe later. But take this customer. He has just paid full list price and he gets to his meeting and brings the boys out to the parking lot to look at his new car. "What'd it cost you, Charley?" somebody asks. And Charley points to the sticker he has left on to show that it is brand new. "What? You must be some idiot to pay the sticker price for a new car these days." So what does Charley think of me? That I embarrassed him and cheated him, and all his friends and lodge brothers know that he is a dummy.

Give a Little and You'll Get a Lot Back

Well, I know that the salesman who takes the full price makes more commission, but I don't think it is worth the risk in most cases. I'll give up the chance to make a couple of hundred extra bucks in exchange for the chance to make a friend of Charley. Because if he starts to write a check for the full amount and I say, "Take off $250," or "I'll throw in doorguard trim and five steel radials for nothing," Charley is going to think I am the greatest thing since sliced bread. And he is going to tell people about me, maybe even about how he started to write a check for the full amount and I, Joe Girard, wouldn't let him.

Now that sticker price is the truth. But you can get into bad trouble with a customer if you let him believe it, even though it is true.

I don't claim to be an automotive engineer. I didn't finish high school, and I wasn't such a superstar during the years I was there. So I don't get too involved with the technical details of the cars I sell. It is not like I am selling tandem-axle, over-the-road trucks to technical people. But sometimes a customer comes in with some technical fact stuck in his head. His brother-in-law told him that if you get a certain rear-axle ratio on the car, you'll save gas. Well, I have checked, and it amounts to pennies. So when a guy asks me if the car has a 3.25 ratio, like he wants, I'll say, "You're right. You sure know your cars, don't you." That serves two purposes. First of all, it makes him feel good. Second of all, it keeps my selling effort from being interrupted by my having to look in the specification book or call the service department or even the factory.

If the customer brings up something that will make a lot of difference, I'll check it out. Because I don't want him ever to think I stiffed him on anything. Not ever. But the axle ratio and stuff like that doesn't matter. I wouldn't tell anybody a polyester suit was 100 percent wool, though. And I wouldn't tell a housewife that a refrigerator was 22 cubic feet when it was only 17. Because people find out about things like that, and then they never forget. And even if they are too ashamed to tell their friends what you did, they will bad-mouth you and your store and your products in some other way. Girard's Law of 250 is always operating.

So we get back to honesty as the best policy, with a little flattery and even a small lie useful in some cases. All you ever get from telling a big lie is a chance to tell your buddies later how you stiffed some mooch. But if that is the kind of kick you get from selling, you're going to dig your own grave sooner or later. And you are going to make it tough for the rest of us who want to make money by making satisfied customers who come back again and again and send in their friends. If you don't believe that, take my word for it. I sell more cars than anybody else in the world, and I believe it.

You never get caught by telling the truth—or making a prospect feel good when you stretch it.

14

Facing the Customer

Ask people to describe the typical car salesman, and chances are they'll tell you he wears the latest fashion suit—this year that means a three-piece European-cut plaid. They'll tell you he wears Bally boots or alligator loafers and a white-on-white shirt. In other words, they'll tell you that the typical car salesman is wearing maybe $500 on his back and on his feet. And that is the way they think of it—expensive. Then they start to think, "This guy is going to make too much money off me."

I make a lot of money, and I have for years. And I like good clothes, and I wear them whenever I can. But one place I do not wear my best clothes is to work. Don't get me wrong. I dress neat and clean. Nothing cheap. But I don't look like I need to hustle you to pay my tailor. I believe a salesman should look as much as possible like the people to whom he sells. I sell Chevrolets, not Mercedes 450s. Millions of people buy Chevrolets every year, but they are not generally your

richest people. And in my area they are mostly working people. They work in the factories and offices around here, and
they work hard for their money, and they aren't in the top
brackets. So if they walk in and are met by a guy with
clothes that look expensive, they get even more scared than
they were before.

We are not talking about poor people. A poor man doesn't
buy a new car, not even the lowest priced Chevette. My customers pay an average of about $5,000 for the cars they buy
from me. But a lot of them have to borrow most of that
money from the bank, the finance company, or their credit
union. They are good credit risks, but they are not high rollers.
And that's how I want them to see me. That's how I want to
look to them, like a guy who is in their bracket and who un-
derstands their economics.

Look Like You're Their Kind of Guy

When they see me for the first time, they relax a little. Because I wear a sport shirt and slacks. I never wear clothes that
will antagonize my customers and make them feel uneasy. I
am not wearing colorless nail polish like a lot of salesmen do
who get a lot of manicures. That puts people off too. Working
guys may have grease under their nails that can't come off, but
they expect a salesman to be clean. You'd think any salesman
would know that. But I've seen some flashy guys in this business who don't seem to have taken a bath in a long time, nail
polish or not. A working guy may not have had time to go to
the sauna after he left the factory, but he has a right to expect
his salesman to take the trouble to be clean. You may think
I'm making too much of this point, but let me assure you that
I'm not. People complain to me about other salesmen. So it's
important.

When a customer comes into my office, he finds a neat
businesslike place that doesn't rub him the wrong way. I know
some guys who decorate their offices with religious pictures

and all kinds of stuff that people consider controversial. If your aunt brought you a blessed picture of the Pope from Rome, that's a real keepsake. But hang it at home. A lot of people, even Catholics, may not think that's the right sort of thing for your offce walls. I put up sales award certificates and plaques, so people will know they are dealing with a top salesman. After all, they think, if this fellow sells so many cars, he must be giving good deals. At least that's what I want them to think, and it's true.

I also keep away from the customer's view things like color charts, brochures showing optional equipment, and anything else that may give a person a chance to pick up something and start worrying about what color or what kind of accessories he should have. He didn't come in to buy a sky-blue car with electric window controls. He came in to buy a car from me, period. All the rest comes later, after he has decided that he wants to buy a car from me. So I don't want to give him an opportunity to start flipping through a book so he can get off the hook by saying that he needs more time to think about everything. And I don't want him to start loading up the car before he has decided that he is going to buy. Because, before you know it, he will want so much that he won't be able to afford anything. And the price will be so high that everybody he calls will be able to give him a lower price, because they won't be quoting a car with wall-to-wall Persian rugs and special-order metallic paint.

Get Them Obligated to You

I don't give my customers a reclining easy chair to sit in either. I want them to relax, but I don't want them to get so comfortable that I can't get through to them. Relaxing them is crucial, of course. But I have a lot more effective ways to relax a customer and get him obligated to me. A comfortable chair won't do that. But other things will.

He starts to pat his pockets looking for a cigarette, and I

ask him what he smokes, because I don't want him to remember that he has cigarettes in the glove compartment of his car and run out to get one. I keep a lot of brands in my office. Whatever he smokes, chances are I've got a pack, and I give it to him. "That's O.K., keep the pack." Wow! Keep the pack! Who tells a customer that? I do. What does it cost? Fifty cents—pretax. And now he is obligated to me. Matches, of course, he gets free. What else? How about a drink? What do you drink? Wine? Scotch? I've got that too. Free! And he won't have to drink alone, because I take out a vodka bottle filled with 100-proof water and drink along with him. I don't want him falling on his face. I just want him relaxed enough to let me help him get what he wants and can afford.

If he brings his kid in, I've got balloons and lollipops for him, and I've got buttons for everybody in the family that say nothing but "I like you." Anything I put in his hands and in his family's hands makes him feel a little obligated to me, not too much but just enough.

Sometimes a person will walk in and start looking at a car on the floor. I'll go over and stay near him, but not too close. Once in a while, a guy will get down on the floor and look underneath. So will I. It may sound crazy, but it is a very good opener. The man sees you just looking with him and maybe he laughs, and you are ready to start working on him. Once in a while somebody will admire the shirt I'm wearing (I like to wear colorful polka dot sport shirts), and I'll say, "You like it. Here. It's yours." And I'll start to take it off. I want him to know that if that's what it will take to make him happy, I'll be glad to give it to him. I keep an extra shirt in my office in case a person actually follows through and takes mine. I think only one ever did. But I'm ready for him. And just the gesture, as a joke, can do a lot to break the ice. Whether we get to that point or not, I want everybody to think I'll do anything for them, even give them the shirt off my back.

I keep my office as neat as possible. There is nothing distracting for the customer to look at and to start thinking about. When we are talking about prices and deals, if I have to look something up or do some figuring on my adding machine, I don't do it where he can look over my shoulder. I keep that stuff on top of a filing cabinet a few feet away from my desk. I am the only one who gets to see the figures and the tape from the machine.

Another thing I always do is clean up after a prospect leaves. I straighten everything, empty the ashtrays, put away the glasses, and spray the place with an air deodorizer. A lot of people don't like the smell of alcohol or smoke. And they don't run into it when they come into my office.

The way I look at it, I am an actor playing a part. I want the stage to be just right for the show I am going to put on, and I want my costume to be exactly right too. What I said about how I dress applies to my kind of customers. I am not saying that you should dress that way if your neighborhood, your customers, and the practices and rules in your area are different. A top salesman is a first-rate actor. He plays a part and convinces his audience—the customer—that he is what he is playing. If your customers are flashy dressers, then you ought to look like them.

I know my customers, and I know what they expect. I know them so well, since most of them ask for me by name and know me, that I can meet them without a shave and know that they'll probably appreciate that. But, however you do it, the thing that matters most is that you know your customers, if not by name at least by style and type. Then you too will be able to disarm them and win the war.

If those first moments of contact with you help them to relax a little, to overcome their fear, and they begin to feel obligated to you for taking up your time, you have already started to win.

Get them with you from the start and they'll stay with you.

15

Selling the Smell

One of the great evangelists of selling once said that, to win, what we have to do is sell the sizzle, not the steak. Well that's exactly what you have to do in selling cars. After all, most of my customers have already owned a car, and maybe even a Chevrolet. And they certainly have seen a lot of cars in their lives. There must be more than 100 million of them on the streets. So a Chevrolet, all by itself, is no big deal to them.

What is a big deal is a shiny new one that will feel good to touch, to sit in, and to own. And the thing about a new car that turns on more people than anything else is its smell. Have you ever noticed the smell of a brand new car? If you were blindfolded, you'd still be able to tell what it was if someone put you in a new car. Touching the car and seeing it make some people drool to own it. But nothing turns people on like the smell.

So I always want to make every customer smell it. I didn't say "let"—I said "make." A lot of people are afraid to get into a new car at first. And they are very reluctant to drive it. That's because they are afraid that they will feel obligated somehow. Which is why I say push them into it if you have to. Because you want them to feel obligated, like they have broken the seal or unwrapped it so they have to buy it.

Once they get in and smell, they want it. That is such an obvious fact that you would think that every salesman who has ever sold even one car would know it. But it is always a subject of sales training meetings, because a lot of salesmen don't think it is worth the trouble. "Why bother? The mooch knows what it's like. All he wants is the right price."

Remember the Smells That Sold You

Anybody who says that doesn't know his own feelings. But I never forget things in my life that excited me the first time. I remember the first time I ever had my hands on a new power drill. It wasn't mine. A kid down the block got it for Christmas. But I was there when he unwrapped it, a new Black and Decker, and I took it from him and plugged it in and couldn't stop drilling holes in everything. And I remember the first new car I was in. I was already grown up, and the only cars I had ever been in were old ones where the upholstery stank sour. But one of the guys in the neighborhood got one after the war, I was in it the first day, and I'll never forget that smell.

When you're selling other things, it may not be quite the same. You sell a man a life insurance policy, and there's nothing you can let him smell or drive. But anything that moves or feels, you've got to let him have some. Who would try to sell a man a cashmere coat without getting him to stroke it first?

So be sure that you put him in the car. I always do. It makes him lust to own it. And even if I lose the sale, I have a shot at getting him back once he has to go back to the smell of his own again. And when I put a man in a new car, I don't say anything to him. I just let him drive it. You'll hear from the so-called experts that this is the time to sell him all the features of your product. But I don't believe it. I find that the less I talk, the more he smells and feels—and starts to talk. And I want him to smell and feel and talk. Because I want to hear what he likes and what he's worried about. I want him to help me qualify him by telling me where he works and something about his family and where he lives. A lot of times, a customer will tell you everything you need to sell him and to get his credit approved just while you are sitting in the passenger seat. And that is a must—letting him drive it.

People like to try things out, to touch them, to play with them. Remember the shock absorber displays they had in gas stations (where you would pull a handle with a worn-out shock and then pull a handle with a new shock)? Well, I'm sure most of you have at one time tried working them. We are curious. No matter what you sell, look for ways in which you can demonstrate your product. The important thing is to be sure that the prospect participates in the demonstration. If you can appeal to their senses, then you are also appealing to their emotions. I'd say that more things are bought through emotions than through logic.

Once he is behind the wheel, chances are he is going to ask you where he should go. I always tell him to go wherever he wants to go. If he lives in the neighborhood, I may suggest that he drive by the house. Then he can let his wife and kids see it. Some neighbor may be out on the porch. I want him to let everybody see him behind the wheel of that new car, because I want him to feel like he has bought that car and is showing it off. That helps lock up his decision, because he may not want to come home and tell everybody he couldn't make a good deal. I don't want to hook a customer too much—just a little.

I don't want the customer to take the car too far, because my time is worth a lot of money. But a person taking a demonstration drive will tend to think it is too far when it really isn't.

So I let a man drive as much as he likes, because if he thinks he has gone a little too far that also helps to make him feel obligated to me.

Getting Him Hooked

When I talk about hooking the customer and making him feel obligated, I don't mean to say I am doing anything bad to the person. There is never a point in the selling situation, even after he signs the order, when he can't say no and back out. So he is on equal terms with me. But I feel that I have a perfect right to assume that if somebody comes into my place of business to see me, he is there because he is interested in buying a car from me. It is my duty to him, as well as to myself, to help him clear up his doubts and fears and buy a car.

When I talk about smell, I really mean it. But it stands for a lot of things besides the smell itself. To me, the smell of a new car stands for the excitement of the experience. I suppose there are people these days who don't get a thrill when they buy a new car. Maybe they have had so many, it doesn't matter to them any more. But for most people, me included, buying something new, even as ordinary as buying a new shirt, is exciting. I want to take it home and put it on and show it off. And there is hardly anything to compare to the excitement of a new car. For a lot of people it is almost like having a baby. They practically want to hand out cigars and send announcements.

It is all part of what I call the smell. That feeling, you could almost say, sells the car by itself. Almost, but not really. Because a lot of salesmen don't understand it, so they don't use it. You have to use it to get it to work for you. You don't just let it happen. You don't just let anything happen if you are a real pro. You make it all happen. You make sure the customer has the opportunity to smell and feel the excitement, the thrill of it all.

I want to add one final word on the value of selling the

smell. In the years just after World War II, new cars were scarce, and a lot of potential new car buyers had to settle for late-model used cars. At that time a product came onto the market that was bought by a lot of used car dealers. That product was a liquid that the dealer sprayed in the trunk and on the floors of late-model used cars. The reason: It made them smell like new cars. But you know the value of that smell, because you certainly remember the first time it hit your nose. So never forget that. Look back into your own experience as a consumer whenever you are selling somebody else. Because we all share a lot of experiences. And if that smell turned you on, you can bet it will turn on almost everybody.

Whatever you sell, there is an equivalent of the smell of a new car. Think of yourself as a customer.

Think of what excites you about a product, or used to when you first bought it. Then use that experience to sell the excitement, the thrill of owning your product.

16

Espionage and Intelligence

In every other kind of war, each side spies on the other and has intelligence agents whose job it is to find out what its side is going up against. In selling, we usually call that *qualifying the customer*. But "qualify" is a word that has a lot of different meanings. One of them is like "eligible." And let me tell you that, as far as I'm concerned, everybody is qualified to buy a car from me. That's why I like to think of this part of the selling job as espionage and intelligence. I want to know what the customer wants to do and what he ought to do and what he can afford to do.

Sometimes all of those things turn out to be the same. But a lot of the time they are different. What the customer wants may not be something he'll be happy with or can afford. I listen to what a customer says he wants, and I try to give it to him. But if I think it won't work for him or that he can't afford it and can afford something better, then I make up my own mind. But how do I know what to try to sell the customer? I look and I listen and I ask.

What I look and listen for are things that will open him up, get him talking, so that he will tell me about himself, his needs, and his ability to pay. But I don't always let him make those decisions. Very often, maybe in a majority of cases, I decide. Because the customer often doesn't really know what he can handle and what he should buy.

Most people don't understand enough about life insurance to know what they need, so they let their salesman decide. When it comes to clothes, people know they want something different, something fashionable, or at least something that won't make them look conspicuous because it is out of style. So the salesperson works it out with them. It's a kind of negotiation, based on what's in style, what's available, and what looks good on them. No clothing salesman in his right mind will sell a person something that will make him look awful. But people can disagree on how someone looks in something. So there is a wide margin for making those kinds of decisions by both customer and salesman.

With a car, it is not quite the same. You don't try very hard to sell a man a two-seat sports car if he has a wife and four kids. If it's his second or third car and he is loaded, it doesn't much matter. But you know that if you manage to push him into a little job when he needs a big one, you have created one very unhappy fellow. And you don't want to do this, no matter how sure he is that he wants that nifty little number.

So you're playing a game with the customer, trying to find out what's best for him no matter what he says. Because what's best for him is best for you, if you want him to speak well of you and come back some day for another one. And don't forget that, at this point, you are dealing with a scared man.

Getting His Name Is Crucial

He walks in the front door, and the first thing I say is, "Hi. My name is Joe Girard." And the very next thing I say is not, "What's your name?" I don't want to scare him any more. I don't want him to start pulling back right away. So instead of asking, I say, "And your name is ..." He won't hesitate a second before he finishes that sentence and tells me his name. Notice that I really didn't ask him. I just didn't give him any reason to see me as somebody trying to dig into his insides. It was natural and casual, and I got his name. From then on, I use it, because we now have a personal relationship. He's Bill and I'm Joe. And if he tries to call me Mister, I let him know that it's Joe. I've broken a little ice.

As I said before, if he starts out by walking around a car on the floor or even crawling under it, so do I. I don't say much, because I want to know a lot, but I want him to give it to me without my prying it out of him.

I may ask him what he's got in mind or what he's driving now, but mostly I'll just be passive and wait for him. He's going to tell me something. And once he starts to talk, I'll stay with him and move with him. But I will never crowd him at this stage of the game. I want to draw him out, let him show himself—like in military intelligence, where you want to let the enemy reveal himself, too much, you hope.

If somebody starts out by asking for me by name, which happens a lot of the time, then I have a good opener. I ask him how he heard about me. He may say he read about me somewhere, and then I'll follow up and ask him where, and we're talking. Or he may give me somebody's name, which I tell him I know even if I never heard of the guy. Or he'll say he heard about me at the plant. What plant? And we'll be talking about where he works. However he answers, I get the conversation to start moving, and maybe I learn something useful, like whom he knows that I know or where he works. If I get a name I know, then I can ask if he lives near the other fellow, and I know something about the neighborhood and can try to figure his income from that. We go from the plant to his job, and that leads to another estimate of his income.

I try to be like a machine that he doesn't notice is turned on, like maybe a recorder or a computer. Because there is nothing he is going to say about a neighborhood or some suburb or a bowling alley or a factory that I can't make him think I know something about. Whatever he says, I've got an answer that is a half question and gets him going some more, and keeps me from getting in too deep about something or some place I don't know very well. While we're going on about his bowling league at the plant and how well his team is doing, I'll spring on him, very casually, this: "Let me have your keys and we'll get an appraisal for you."

Notice that I don't ask, "Do you have a car to trade in?" I don't want to ask that question, because it will start him thinking in wrong directions. He'll start to figure that if he says yes, he'll be going too far into a deal. Or he may want to lie and say no, because he figures that he should get my best price and then spring the trade on me to get maybe an even better price on the trade-in allowance. It doesn't work that way, of course. You get as much as we can give you, as much as the book says, no matter when we figure in the value of the trade-in. But a lot of people figure they can play another game if they hold off.

What I want to do is get him involved without his awareness, in a way that makes it a little harder for him to start throwing up barriers against me.

I have to catch him quick. Otherwise he'll work all the dodges. You watch him when he tries to say he doesn't have a trade, and you can usually tell from his eyes if he is telling the truth or trying to play games. I mean, there are people who want to give the old car to their father or their kid who has just reached driving age, but mostly they want to trade the old one for the new one. So I cut through all the dodges by saying, "Give me the keys."

These days I don't usually look at the trade-ins, because I have somebody working for me who does that. I'll discuss the way I use extra help later and, more important, how most salesmen in this sort of business can't afford not to use extra help. But for a long time I looked over the trade-ins—and sometimes I still do.

How to Read a Customer

An experienced salesman can read a customer, his house, his car like a book. Most people don't notice what other people are wearing or where they live or what they drive. But if you pay attention to details, like how shiny the elbows are and things like that, you can learn a lot. I can walk around and look inside a person's car and tell you everything about it and about its owner.

There are obvious things, like how many miles on the speedometer, and the number of service station stickers on the doorjamb and their mileage. Obviously, they tell me how much driving the man does in a year and how carefully he takes care of his car. Now those things tell you directly about the value of the car. If he gets it serviced often, it tells you he is a careful person. If his mileage is way above average, I've got something to talk about with him. I can ask if he travels a lot or has gone on some very long vacation trips. When I look in the front seat and in the glove compartment of the car, I'm looking for brochures from other dealers and makes. They will tell me as much as anything what kind of car he has been looking for and how many different prices he has been quoted. From that, I get a pretty clear idea of how low I have to go to get him.

If his tires are badly worn, I know he is facing an outlay of $150 or more for a new set. That puts him a long way down the road to a new car, because a lot of people start figuring that they might as well go all the way as spend a big hunk of change on nothing but a set of tires. When I open the trunk to look at his spare tire and I find fishing tackle, I have something else to talk about. Fishermen love to talk about where they fish and what they have caught. And if I see a trailer hitch on the rear end that tells me even more about him. He is a camper or a boater.

Now if his car is an obvious junker, I have to be careful. He may not have enough miles on it to get home, which is great for me to know, because it means he pretty much has to buy a car right away. But I can't tell him that. A man's car is like his wife; he can knock it all he wants to, but as soon as some-body else tries to, he gets insulted. So I'll be very careful about what I say if the car is a dog. Mostly, I tell him it looks really good considering the mileage or the age.

Another thing I keep an eye out for is windshield and bumper stickers. Political stuff I say nothing about, because politics is not something you can talk about with a customer without getting into trouble. If my own son were running for President, I wouldn't wear a Girard for President button to work. But I want to talk about the other kinds of stickers that resorts put on or that you get when you go to national parks and other tourist attractions. Because wherever that guy has been, I have been. Even if I never heard of the place, I'll find some way to use it to break some more ice. And if there is a baby seat or any toys, bike carriers, sleeping bags, or anything else, I have learned something about the man, his needs and interests, and the way he treats the things he owns.

Zeroing In

When I get back to him, I'll say, "You keep that car in good shape." That gets us past questions about how much I'm going to allow him on it and makes him feel I like it. Now maybe I'll ask him, "What did you have in mind?" And then we start to go. He may say he wants another one just like it. Maybe he complains that it rattles too much. So I'll suggest a two-door instead of a four-door. They do rattle a little less and, better than that from my standpoint, they cost a little less, so I can quote him a lower price than he may have got from someone else on a four-door.

If you're selling houses and a guy complains about all the lawn mowing he had to do, you aren't going to suggest a place with a huge yard. If he complains about walking up all the stairs, you won't offer him a three-floor colonial; you'll come up with a one-floor ranch house. Same thing with cars. You are going to put him into something that carries his family, hauls his boat, and fits his pocketbook.

But if I sense that a customer is choking up, I won't keep driving to a close. I'll back off a little. Maybe I'll pick up on the carseat I saw in his car and ask him how old his baby is. He'll probably bring out the pictures in his wallet and I'll look and lavish praise. Unless he asks me, I'm not going to talk about my family. This is not a social situation. This is selling, and I believe that one of the dumbest things that salesmen can do is compete with a customer. He brings out pictures of the kids, and a lot of salesmen will bring out pictures of their kids. That's not the smartest thing you can do, because you're trying to top him. When you do that, you're saying, "You think that's something, look at mine."

He doesn't care about your kids' pictures. He wants to show off his. What good do you accomplish by competing? None at all. Let him have the stage. Just sit there and look.

If I see fishing tackle in the car, I'll ask him about where he's been fishing lately, and pretty soon he'll tell me about a fish he caught that was this big. I hear some salesmen come right back with "That's nothing. I caught one *that* big last Sunday." So what? So you've made him think that maybe the biggest event in his life isn't worth talking about. Maybe you caught a forty-foot white shark named Jaws. But, like I said, this isn't a bragging contest at the local bowling alley. This is business, and if all he caught was a minnow, make him think it was the whale that swallowed Jonah. You want to bring him over to your side and beat him. But if you do it with fishing statistics, he'll turn against you and wriggle off the hook.

I've already discussed the importance of the demonstration ride. You're giving him a piece of the merchandise. A free sample, and you want to give him enough so that he'll want it all. I want him to take a ride so that he'll want it all. I want him to take a ride so that he'll feel he has got something for nothing and owes me a little something. And I want him in the car so that he can take it somewhere, and his kids and his friends and his co-workers can see him in it. That makes it a little harder for him to go back to driving his junker. And I want him in that car because I want to see where he goes and hear everything he wants to say about it, including what he doesn't like, if anything.

But most of all, as I have said before, I want him to get that smell way up into his sinuses and into his brain, because then I'm getting him hooked on it. And that is when it gets very hard to go back to the stale smell of his clunker out there on the street.

When he has got that full treatment and is still with me, we go into the office, the door is closed, and no phone calls are allowed to interrupt the next steps. We are still talking and feeling each other out. When I finish looking at his car, I may ask, "It's paid for, isn't it?" If he says he's got a couple of payments left, I know that he is a credit customer and that my ability to arrange financing and get the monthly payments right for him may be more important than total price. We may talk a lot about total price, but what he may care most about is, "How much a month?"

Credit Is the American Way

That is the fact with most big-ticket items for most people. And there's nothing for a customer to be ashamed of. Everybody buys on installments. That's the American Way. If you wait till you have it all in the bank, you may wait all your life for nothing. But a lot of people are still a little ashamed that they don't pay cash for everything. So you have to handle it carefully, especially if the customer has been paying over a very long period, and has hardly any equity in the car even though it is almost all paid up.

Sometimes my ability to sell a customer at all depends on my ability to get him enough credit to let him pay for the car. If he is really strapped or has had a tax lien or a recent bankruptcy, I can still find ways to get him the money to buy the car, but if that's the case I have to know about it. Because that changes the nature of the deal. Price is out the window. Now all we are talking about is finding a way to get credit for the customer: whether we have to get a co-signer or, in some cases, even put the car in a friend's name. We'll go into the way I get a friend to co-sign a note for a customer later. And using the device of putting the car in somebody else's name requires great care. If you are going to resort to that, the thing you have to be sure of is that you tell the bank or finance company in advance that this is what you are doing. Otherwise you are not obeying the law. They have to know in advance, because they have to know where to find the car if they ever have to repossess.

The important thing about credit is that you want to know as soon as possible whether you have to sell the customer on price or on your ability to find him the money, regardless of price. There is no sense in dancing around the price if his credit rating is zero.

But if his car is paid for or nearly paid for, we've got no problems. And as soon as I have found out that he's O.K., I start chipping away at his natural fear again. I'll maybe pick up on the Yellowstone Park sticker he's got on the window. I ask him about the trip and listen. If he asks if I've been there, I'll probably say yes, but I'm still going to let him tell me, not me tell him, because I want to let him talk about something he enjoyed, something pleasant, so that he'll relax.

I know when the customer is relaxing, because I read his body language. I watch his face, his eyes, the way he holds his arms close to him, and his legs crossed tight until he starts letting loose a little. While all of this is going on, I am finding out what he needs and what he can be sold. There are enough different models, sizes, trim, accessories so that I can figure out a car that has just about any price it takes to sell him, just so long as it will do the job for him. I can trade him up to a Monte Carlo or down to a Vega or even a Chevette from the Impala he has been thinking about. Of course, I'd like to make it easy and sell him exactly what he has in mind when he walks in. But he may not be able to afford that. Or he may really be able to afford something bigger and better. I can go either way.

What I need to know is how much shopping he has already done and what prices have been quoted to him. I need to know this because I am probably going to get him by making him think he is getting the best possible price from me. I don't mean that he won't. He will, if I can help it, because I'd rather make a little less per car and sell a lot of them than be a hog and just sell a few. That's the philosophy, that's the system that has made me the world's greatest salesman. I take in more than any other car salesman does because I want to sell more cars, not get higher prices. Do that and the rest takes care of itself. And, of course, you send out a happy customer who talks you up wherever he goes and sends back even more business.

If I know that he has brochures from other dealers in his car or I see them in his pocket, I know he already has prices in mind. But even if I don't know that, I can find it out easily. By this time we are in my office. I've given him a drink or a cigar. If his kids came in with him, they've got balloons and lollipops. I've played with the kids, even got on my knees to talk to them if necessary. No problem. My office floor is clean, and besides, I can buy a few pairs of slacks with the commission from just one sale. So it's worth it.

A lot of salesmen will get to their desk and put a blank pad on top. That way, they figure, they can write down all the information about the customer and the car they are selling him. It's a nice system, they figure. Wrong! It's a dumb system, because if you do that, and then you get the guy close to the end, you can't finish him off.

Getting Ready for the Close

What I do is always keep a blank order form and a credit application on my desk. Then, as we talk and I get information about the customer and where he lives and what he does and what he wants, that goes right on the forms. Then if I get him right up to the finish, I've got a filled-in order and all I need is a signature. The other way you've got to transfer all the information from the pad to the forms. And while you're doing that, the guy can remember that he's got to buy a collar button before the jewelry store closes. And he runs and you've lost him.

I'm not saying you should lock the door and take the doorknob off to keep the customer there. I don't play it that way. But when we have got to that point in the process, I have spent an hour or more of my own and my associates' time. And that is worth a lot of money to me. And it damned well ought to be to the customer. If he came that far and his intentions weren't serious, he is a bad guy. Of course, if I couldn't meet the legitimate price of somebody else, which is unlikely, or I didn't have a car anywhere near what he wanted, which is practically impossible, the person has a perfect right to leave without buying. Because if that happens, it means I haven't done my job professionally.

If I lose a customer at that point, it means I have done something wrong. We all know that you can't sell them all. We all know that some people come in just because they have nothing else to do. But if you assume that about anybody without going over the whole thing in your mind to find out what you did wrong, you will not be doing the proper job of training and retraining yourself. You have to assume that you are guilty of bad selling until proven innocent by your own self-examination.

But the commonest reason for losing a customer who seemed really interested is not listening enough, not watching the face and the body movements of the customer. If you don't spend enough time and concentration on that, you are going to miss something that the guy is telling you without trying to tell you. And that something probably has to do with why he is afraid, why he is hesitating, and what you are not doing to get him over the last hurdles.

Everybody hates silence, and most people want to jump out of silence. Let your customer do that. Let him talk because he can't stand the silence. Let him offer you the clues to his hesitation and reluctance. You can learn a lot more by watching and listening than you can by talking.

But there are moments when the salesman can gain by talking. The guy is uneasy, he's twitching, smiling foolishly, tapping his toes, doing all those things that people do when they are uncomfortable and afraid. You watch and you notice, and you figure he really has a bug up him. But you don't know what it is. You have found out what he needs and what he can afford, but you aren't moving him toward a close. It's quiet. Nothing is happening except his unease. So you ask a question. That is sometimes a pretty good way to get an answer. But you don't ask him a question that he can answer yes or (especially) no. You don't ask, "Is there anything else you want to know?" Because he can say no, and you've blown it. You ask something he has to answer with real words: "What have I left out?" "What didn't I tell you that you need to know to make up your mind?" Or even something as direct as: "What did I do wrong?" That can make a customer feel he should help *you*. And you can start getting hold of him then.

When I talk about nailing down a customer at this point,

I don't mean closing him. There really is no sharp line between qualifying and closing, of course. We talk about them as separate things, but if you are handling your selling situation properly, there is a smooth flow from one step to the next. You know when the intelligence phase is over, because you know what the customer really wants and needs and can afford to buy. If you know all that—and know that you know it—you are at the next step.

Let the customer reveal himself, while you watch and listen, and he'll lay himself open for the close.

17

Locking Them Up

A lot of salesmen lose sales because they move too hard too soon. They start pushing a pen in the guy's face before they know anything about him and what he wants. So they chase him away no matter how bad he really wants to buy. And a lot of salesmen start to close without having a clear sense of their own want.

I told you about the bag of groceries and how I put an image of that bag in place of that customer's face. I really did that. It worked, because it drove me to be better and to fight harder for that sale. The reason was simple: I knew what I wanted. And I always know what I want when I come up against a customer. We all want so many things that it should never be a problem to define your own want for every sale. Sometimes all I want is that sale because it will put me ahead of yesterday. I know myself and I know how much the competition of the game means to me. If I am not fighting against somebody else's record because I'm so far ahead of everybody else, then I'm wanting to beat Joe Girard.

When you close the door and confront that customer alone, it's like you are a surgeon with a patient on the operating table. But you're not going to start cutting until you're sure of what you have to do. You don't want to take out his gall bladder if he has appendicitis. So, when you start your close, you had better be sure that you have done the whole intelligence job. When you know what the customer wants that you can give him and when you know what you want, then you're ready to go.

Assuming the guy didn't come in because his wife threw him out of the house and he had nothing else to do, I figure I've got a live one every time somebody walks into my office and I close that door.

Moving Him Along Past the Sticking Point

We're talking models now. "So you liked that four-door Impala," I tell (not ask) him. He may still be trying to wriggle out. But I assume he wants to buy, but is just getting a little more scared because that door is closed. Maybe this is the time when I offer him a drink or a cigar. "What color was it that you wanted?" I may say. If he mentions a color, I assume we are past the point of no return. Maybe the question of color comes early when somebody is buying a suit. I need a *blue* suit, a man may say. But at the beginning he says he needs a car, not a green Caprice. So when we get to the point where he or I talk color, I am closing him whether he knows it or not.

"A tan one this time. Hang on a minute, please." And I'm out the door to check the inventory list. At least that's what he thinks. And then I'm back. "We just happen to have one," I tell him. "They're pulling it out for you." I've got the order written up already, because I have been doing it as we go along. "Just O.K. this," I say, pushing the pen into his hand. I don't say, "Sign here." That's too formal. "Just O.K. this." And maybe he does, and that can be the end of it.

But we all know that it generally doesn't go that easily. And I won't push a pen at a customer too soon. But if we have talked color or he has asked for specific optional equipment and I have found a car in stock that has what he wants, I have to go to the next step.

That next step is the big one, but it is the one that gets us both on the same side. They tell you in the training sessions that the lockup starts with asking for the order. But for me it is asking for money. I get up and almost turn my back on the customer, and very straight out, I half turn, put out my hand, and say, "Give me $100 and I'll have them get the car ready for you." I don't hesitate and say, "Well, I'll need a deposit." That's no good, because it just puts you on the edge. I want to put us way into the middle of the next plateau.

I've asked for $100, so he has to come up with a reason why we don't go ahead. Maybe he pulls out his wallet and says, "All I've got is $73." And do you know what I say then? Sure you do. I tell him $73 is fine. Now he says that he needs some walking-around money, so I settle for $60 or even $50. But not much less, because if he has come this far, we both want him to buy the car. And if he puts down at least $50—maybe even a little less sometimes—he is going to buy.

But what if he looks in his pocket and has only $27 in cash? "I'll take a check," I assure him. But I want $100 or more, if he is going to lay a "reader" on me. Now a lot of people are happy to write a check, because they figure that they can stop payment on it if they change their mind.

How to Make Sure You Get Paid for Your Time

Think about it for a minute. I have spent maybe an hour or more with somebody who has come in and asked for me and tells me he wants to buy a car. And I believe him. So when he writes a check to hold that car, I assume he is serious about it, which means he wants me to have that money. I am not joking. I am not in business for the fun of it—though I love my profession. So when I get that check, I excuse myself a minute, go out the door, and start the process of "hammering" (certifying) that check. A check is money that, I assume, he wants me to have. And I am going to get it as fast as I can.

One thing he can count on is getting his car when he needs it. If our conversation has covered his travel and vacation plans, I know that he is leaving on a trip in two days. He'll have a car, as near to what he wants as there is in the whole area, when he needs it. As I have said, if we don't have one in our stock, another dealer in the community certainly will. And, since we all have an interchange arrangement, I can always deliver him pretty much what he wants. I assume that he is serious about his need, so I am always willing to go out on a limb and have a car ready when I say I will.

After all, we are in the business of buying and selling. So when I get money, a customer gets a car. Sometimes I can't find what he wants. That's very rare, but it happens. Though I still assume that what he wanted most was a car, not a certain kind of radio or a particular transmission. I can't believe that a customer gets to the point of handing over a check and signing an order only because he wants a vinyl roof cover. I assume he wants an automobile. This he will get, and he will get good value whatever the price he pays.

If you think that most of my selling has less to do with color trim than price, you are correct. I deal in a commodity. A lot of things make what I sell different from what my competitor could not sell the same customer. Some of it has to do with me and the fact that I get the customer to like me and trust me. We have talked about all the different ways I use to get him to relax and to trust me. But if a customer works hard for his money, he knows a lot about what the car will cost. He has talked to his friends and he has probably talked to other car salesmen. So when he sees me, he expects to get a lower price than anybody else has quoted him. And I have to believe that

I meet or beat my competitors' prices a lot of the time; my statistics prove this. After all, as I keep saying, if I am selling more cars and trucks than anybody else, I must often be meeting and beating their prices. People may buy from me because they like me and trust me. But that's because they know that they get a fair shake from me.

I have explained before that there is a very broad price range among all the different cars that can meet a customer's needs. Every salesman knows a lot about that. But I believe that I understand this better than anybody else does, because I spend a lot of time studying that part of the job. I know all the different options cars come equipped with from the factory, and I know just about everything that can be installed on a car after we have it in stock. That allows me more price flexibility than just about anybody else in the car-selling business, because I know not only all the different ways a car can be equipped, but I also know all about the costs and selling prices of the options. There are many kinds of optional features that make a car more appealing without adding much to the cost. I said cost, not price. So I can "throw in" for nothing or for very little extra a lot of features that can make my deal all but impossible to beat.

Does that mean I can't ever be beaten? Certainly not. There are a lot of other smart and aggressive salesmen in this and every other business. But if they are not selling 1,500 or even 1,000 cars a year, I have to believe they aren't quite as good as I am. Besides, if I give somebody a price and he takes my price to another dealer, I may lose the sale because of envy. The other salesmen I work with are mostly friends of mine. But those at other dealerships are sometimes jealous of me and will sell a car so cheap that they lose money, just so they can say they beat Joe Girard.

That means, as I am sure you understand, that we are all in this game for more than money. But when somebody sells too cheap just to beat me, he is in it for the wrong reasons. When I say "more than money," I mean money plus other reasons.

But the name of the game is money, and unless the money is there or will be coming in later, I won't sell a car too cheap just to beat the competition. (I've already explained why it is sometimes good business to lose money on one deal in order to get that customer to talk me up, if he's important enough.)

When I describe the range of prices and options, people say that it must get confusing. It is. If a customer tries to keep track of all the elements in the total selling price, he is never going to make it, because he never can know what all those elements cost the dealer or the salesman. For instance, if a dealer sells enough cars during a model year, he becomes eligible for rebates from the factory on all the cars that he has sold during the year, depending on how many he buys from the factory. A customer can never know about that, so he never really knows the cost of a car. Therefore he can't know what the right selling price should be.

Trusting Me After the Sale Is What Counts

What it all comes down to is one word: trust. If a customer trusts me, he will buy from me. But I have to be sure that his trust lasts beyond the moment when he gets his car and pays for it. I have to be sure that he trusts me after he has driven the car home and to work and showed it and talked about it to everybody he knows, including how much he paid me for it.

I have certain factors working for me to build his trust. For one thing, as I keep saying, if I sell more than anybody else, it must be because I know how to quote low prices for the cars I sell. For another thing, people like to brag about how cheaply they buy cars, so they always cut a few dollars off the price they actually paid when they start to talk about it. Besides that, I try to make a friend out of every customer, whether I sell him or not. So the buyer always has the feeling that if anything goes wrong with the car, not only General Motors and Merollis Chevrolet, but Joe Girard stands behind the sale.

When we get to the point of negotiating the price of the car, we are pretty close to the end. But nowhere near all the way. The deposit, if it is big enough, pretty much closes the door on the sale. I have said that I try to get enough cash or a certified check to keep the customer from walking away after he has made a deal. I mean that if I have to take only $10 or $25, the sale is in danger no matter what the customer signs. Because if he takes the Joe Girard deal somewhere else, some hot-air salesman who wants to prove he is a faster gun than I am may undercut my price enough so that the customer is willing to lose his small deposit. You never know for sure that a customer is sold until he has the product and you have all the money.

You know my attitude about the odds. Even though I believe that I am the best, most aggressive salesman in the business, I don't like to let a customer get away only partly sold. This means that if a customer is going to finance his purchase somewhere else than through us, I don't want him to go out the door without first leaving a big deposit or taking the car with him.

Give Him the Product to Close Him

That's right. If for any reason of time or paperwork he is going to leave me without the whole deal being completed or his leaving a lot of his money, I will try to let him take the car he is going to buy.

It's called spot delivery, and it means what it says. I am going to find the car he wants or one almost the same and let him take it home as though it were his own. That may sound pretty risky to you, but in my experience it has proved to be an effective way to stop a customer from looking elsewhere. And you can believe me when I say it works out financially for me and for my dealer.

I'm sure you can see the value of spot delivery. The customer has the car, he takes it home, it's his, even though the final details of financing and registration have not been completed. It's his car. He shows it to his wife, his kids, his neighbors, his friends, his bowling team, his co-workers, his boss, his grocer—everybody sees him in his new car. Then look at the other side of it. I have given him the keys, and he has taken the car away and put miles on it. He may have it for two or three days before the deal is finally closed. Does he think I have given him the use of a brand new car just because I love him? Does he really believe he is under no obligation to me when he is putting 100 or 150 miles on a car that is not his yet? Most important, does he think that he is free to shop for a better deal somewhere else now that he is driving a car that is not really his yet?

He does not. The question of ownership may be a little confusing to him. If he thinks he already owns the car, then I have made the sale. But if he merely thinks that he is borrowing it and is obligated to return it in its original condition, he is correct, and I have not quite clinched the sale yet. But what is he really likely to do once I have put him into that car? Not go driving around the countryside looking to save another $50. Because when he takes the car out, he signs a paper that guarantees that he will return it in its original condition if the transaction, for any reason, does not go through. This is not what a lawyer would call an iron-clad contract, but it is a strong moral bond on any reasonably decent human being. At least it has always worked that way with my customers.

I don't know what the law is where you operate, and I would certainly check it out before I started spot delivery along these lines. But frankly, if you can do it, I don't know of a better way to nail down sales to people who might otherwise be "just looking" long after they should have made up their minds. If I were in the clothing business, I would bring in the tailor and have him start making chalk marks on the sleeves while the customer is still looking in the mirrors and checking the color in the daylight.

When you buy insurance, the agent almost always spot delivers the coverage with a *binder,* which is a short-term policy that you get when you put up just a few bucks toward the full premium. In a way, you are covered even though they haven't checked what you told them on your application, and they don't even know if your check is good. But they must gain more than they lose by that. And so do I—a lot more—because I stop the guy. I end his search for a better price. He doesn't listen to the smartass at the office who tells him, "You paid too much. I could have got it for you wholesale."

But I get much more than that. I give the customer an offer he can't refuse, and he can hardly back out of it later, because I seem to be trusting him with more than anybody else. When I reach back at a person in the office and say, "Give me $100 and I'll get the car ready for you," sometimes the guy will say he doesn't have any cash on him and won't have enough in the bank till payday. If he checks out and has a good job and sounds responsible, I'll look him in the eye and say, "You don't need any money. Your word is good enough for me."

Now how do you think a customer feels when I say that, a customer who is still a little uneasy and hasn't quite made up his mind? That's right: It dissolves all his hesitation, and I've got him.

Or he tells me that he doesn't think the credit union will O.K. his loan till Friday, and it's Wednesday. That would give him two days out there with the sharks. Well, maybe the loan officer at the credit union is one of my birddogs. If he is, I'm sure we can get the wheels to turn a little faster. But even if I don't know him, but the customer looks good, I'll want to put him into "his" car right away.

Now supposing that the customer starts in with a list of specifications that I can't match exactly from stock. A lot of salesmen will say, "Don't worry. You'll get what you want. I'll special-order it from the factory." Not me. If I've got a car in stock that is close enough to what he thinks he wants, I'm going to do everything in the world, including spot delivery, to get him to buy that car. Special orders take weeks, usually longer than you tell the customer. He starts getting itchy, the promised date passes, and he is somewhere else buying a car from some other salesman. I won't ever risk that if I can help it. There are a lot of other cars that will serve his purpose just as well.

Whatever he asks for, I've got. I'm not going to shove him physically into something he hates and then lock him in. But a car in the hand, for him as well as for me, is worth 20 on the come.

Now suppose that I lead the customer out back to where they have prepared the spot-delivery car. He looks and says, "I wanted gray, not powder blue." I tell him how great it looks, and how it's the latest style, and how it will take a week to get a car that is no different from this one except for this one small detail. Meanwhile, he is holding the keys in his hand. Maybe I am also pretending to curse the office staff for making this mistake. Now if the guy stamps his foot and says nothing doing, I want what I want, maybe you've got a problem. But it's not like your wife's dress. You're inside the car most of the time, and besides, none of the colors that Chevrolet paints a car are bad colors.

If you are not in the car business you may think, "Now that's a dirty trick." I didn't always understand selling—in fact, when I first started I was rather naïve. But after selling over 12,000 cars and trucks I understand this business a little better. Let's suppose that a customer wants a silver Monte Carlo with all the options. Now, I have one in stock with all the goodies he wants—only it's light blue. So I order one from the factory. That means it may be many weeks before he takes delivery. In the meantime a friend tells him he should have bought an Oldsmobile Cutlass. So he goes and looks at one. Maybe he decides to buy that instead of my Monte Carlo. He might decide to take a vacation to Hawaii and cancel the car so he'll have the money for the trip. Perhaps his daughter announces she is getting married and he decides he needs the money for the wedding. I've had them tell me their mother-in-law is moving in with them and they need the money to finish off the attic. The car will have to wait till next year. Believe me, I've heard every possible reason for cancelling a car that is on order. Let me explain another facet of selling cars. When a customer decides to buy a new car, the first and most important factor is the car (that's the make-style-options); the second factor is price (Is it a good price? Can I afford it?); and the third, and least important factor is the color. Some may know exactly what color they want. Others may only think they want a certain color. Often a person will come in thinking he would like a white car, but when he sees a brown one he decides he would rather have it in brown. In the case of the customer who wanted the silver Monte Carlo, if I had had the light blue one cleaned and ready, the odds are that the customer would have been just as happy with that one— because it was there, he would not have to wait, and he could take it home with him that very day. What the customer buys is a car at a good price. The color has no bearing on the value he is receiving for his money. My advice to any salesman is to deliver your goods into the hands of your customer as soon as possible after he has made the decision to buy. It will make you both much happier.

Remember: Before I put somebody in a car with no money in my hand, I know a lot about him. We have been sitting, and he has been talking a lot and I have been asking a little. I know where he works and for how long, where he lives and maybe how much of the house is his. I won't put a new car into the hands of a guy who looks and sounds like a deadbeat. What about a con man? you ask. But you have forgotten that the customer hasn't come in to steal a car from me. He is reluctant and I am trying to break down his reluctance by giving him what he really wants in a way that will make up his mind for him. Nobody is going to outfigure me on a thing like that.

And look at the record: I have never been hustled on a spot delivery.

Think again about the effect of a spot delivery. Listen to what a customer says when I put him into a car. "You mean you'd give me the car without me getting an O.K. from the bank?" When I tell him, "Your word is good enough for me," I own him. Of course, just before he takes off, I casually ask him for the name of the insurance company that covers his car, because he's insured in our car too. And don't forget that we have his car in our lot, and that's worth something too. I wouldn't do spot delivery unless I was sure that it was a sound risk and a good investment. If anything happens to the car, he knows it is not his and that he's responsible. But I'm no lawyer, so check out how it works in your area.

Spot Delivery Works for Lots of Salesmen

If you sell things other than cars, spot delivery may work for you even better than it does for me. I once ran into a fellow who serviced and sold TV sets, and he worked spot delivery very effectively. Say you called him up to ask him to come fix your set. What's wrong with it? he asks. The guy says the picture is getting dim and you can hardly see it. He asks how old, what make, and so on. Then he says he'll be right over and he'd like to bring a TV set that the family can use while the other one is in the shop.

You can figure out how it works from there. Chances are the customer's set is an old black and white worth $20 today, and maybe it needs an $80 picture tube. In its place, the TV man has put maybe a $500 color set. Wow! Color! It takes a couple of weeks to fix the other set, and the family is going ape over this "loaner." Only you can bet it is not going to turn out to be a loaner. Who wants to go back to a beat-up old black and white after he's seen some crook bleeding in color. Now my friend is not about to leave a color set with somebody who lives in a tent or has his suitcases packed when he gets there. He is doing a credit check during that first phone call and when he gets to the house.

When the old set is ready, so is an installment purchase agreement that lets the customer trade the black and white for the color set for maybe only $20 a month. Who in that family is going to let Daddy turn down that offer and take back the old set?

I do it, and this TV man does it. You can do it with practically anything but a steak dinner. The first tuxedo I ever owned was sold to me by the man I went to rent one from; he pulled a brand new one out of stock and started marking it up with chalk. I kept saying that I only wanted to rent it for a wedding, and he told me not to worry, because he needed to put another new one my size in his rental stock. He must have had me figured out pretty good, because it made me feel very good to know I was wearing a brand new one that fitted me perfectly just for the price of a rental. When I picked it up after it was altered, I tried it on again to make sure it was right. He put me into the shirt and tie and cummerbund, the whole bit, and it looked great. So guess what happened? He starts in with how many kids do I have, and how many other kids in the family. And before you know it, he has "proved" to me that with so many weddings in the next few years, I couldn't possibly afford to rent as cheaply as I could buy this mohair and silk job, "and look at the fit!"

They say that salesmen can be sold easier than most people, and maybe that's true, but what that tuxedo rental guy showed me happened to be true. And even if it hadn't worked out with the figures, what I paid for the suit at least saved me the trouble of having to go and rent one every time I needed to go to a wedding or a banquet.

When I talk about using spot delivery to sell, you might think I am avoiding price. That's true enough. I pride myself on giving the best deals around and I have that reputation. But, as I have said again and again, the whole business of comparing prices of cars is nearly impossible for a customer because of the tremendous range of differences between models and options. There are even some colors that cost more than others.

The point is that almost no two cars that come out of the factory have exactly the same price. It is possible to have two identical cars, but it almost never happens in the same area at the same time. What this means is that if a customer who has been shopping around comes in to see me with a price, the price I quote him can almost never be for exactly the same car. So there is confusion, and there is leeway. I don't try to confuse him. I don't have to. If I quote him a price much lower, it will be for a couple of reasons. Either the car I have, which may be very similar, costs less, or I am willing to make less on the car I sell him, or both. The fact is that, because I sell so many cars, I can afford to make less on each one. A lot of salesmen shoot for high profit per car because they don't know what I know about building a big flow of prospects. They don't understand that if you have 10 or 12 people coming in every day asking for you, you can make a lot more money by giving better deals than if you see only two or three a day.

There are times when I can't close a customer, and I'll tell him to go out and shop two other dealers. I'll tell him that I think I can beat their price by $500. Well, that may be stretching it a little. But I don't chain the guy to the wall. I let him go out, because I know he is going to come back. When he does, he has to tell me the prices he got at the other dealers'. Otherwise, I tell him, I don't know how to compare. Once I know the prices he has got from others, I can either beat them or not. It is very unlikely that I can chop $500 off his lowest bid. Once in a while, a customer just might get two very high quotes, maybe too high because the salesmen were greedy and they thought they had a mark. But usually I can come in $30 or $50 under his lowest bid.

The guy hears my price and says, "But you told me you

could quote me $500 less and all you give me is $50 less." Well, I am quoting on a car with extra equipment, and I point that out to him. Or I may say, "Look, I didn't know you were such a good shopper. You got the two lowest prices in town already. I just can't cut any more than I have." And that's probably true. O.K., I told him $500, and that brought him back. Now I'm quoting just $50 off. Am I going to lose him? Probably not. I flattered him by telling him how good a shopper he was. And besides, there is an old Chinese proverb: *$50 is $50.* I'll get him for that.

The Magic Words

What the customers want to hear are my magic words: "I got your deal beat." And in the case of almost every person who shops around first, I can make those words good. I certainly *want* to every single time. Because I want to sell a car, even if it cuts my commission a little. After all, a small piece of something is better than a big piece of nothing, and the numbers are good enough in my business to make it worthwhile for me to beat somebody else's price legitimately as often as I can. Earning money makes me very happy. Saving money makes the customer very happy. I beat the customer's best price and everybody is happy.

Sometimes getting the price down enough is not just a matter of cutting the margin and my commission by a few more dollars. Sometimes, in order to quote a low price, I may have to talk a customer out of something optional like a bigger engine ("What do you want a gas burner like that for?") or a certain rear-axle ratio ("It'll save you no more than 50¢ a year on gas") or air conditioning ("It'll cost you about $50 every time you need it, because how many days does it really get that hot around here?").

But whatever I do to sell a customer, he knows he got a square deal when he leaves with that car. Nobody has ever accused me of misrepresenting what I sell. Nobody ever left Merollis Chevrolet with a deal from me where he thought he had bought something that he didn't get. My reputation is worth too much for me to do that. And that's true for most of the salesmen I have ever known in this business, no matter what people say.

Sometimes salesmen are tempted to play games with a customer on financing and payments. It is the worst thing you can do, but it is not hard these days. For a lot of customers, the problem of total price is secondary to the question: How much a month? O.K., now just think of how it can work. A customer wants a certain model. The salesman senses that the man doesn't care about anything but monthly payments. So instead of trying to sell him a car he really can afford, he loads it up with extras. When it comes to setting up the car loan, the customer says he'd like to pay about what he did last time, maybe $93 a month. The salesman says, "We'll get it close." And when the payment book arrives from the bank later, the monthly payments are $135. If the customer signed the thing because he trusted the salesman, he is in trouble. But so is the salesman, because he has hurt a person very badly in the pocketbook for maybe three or even four years. Nobody buys only one car in his life. But that salesman will sell that customer only once, and he will be bad-mouthed to 250 other people.

I don't want that to happen to me. That's why, when they have made their deal with me, my customers always know exactly what they bought for how much a month for how many months. Sometimes a salesman will give the customer the payments he asks for, but make it for four years instead of two. If the customer knows what he is getting when he signs, that's fair. But if it hits him in the face for the first time only when he gets that fat payment book from the bank, then the salesman has hurt him.

I am not saying there is anything wrong with trading a

customer up. I'll do it if I can. Sometimes I'll call a customer at home after he has made his deal, trying to sell him some extras that he might want on the car, such as a better radio or rustproofing or a better set of tires. But he will know what he is getting, and if he says no, it's no. As for payments, I may tell a customer that what he wants is going to cost more. And if he wants to pay it off over the same period as the last car, he may have to refigure his budget and give up something, because the payments are going to be more. Or maybe with the same payments, the term of the loan will run another six months or a year. That's part of selling. If the man can't handle it, I don't want him to take it. Because I don't want that man to have the car repossessed, for then I have lost him and his friends and relatives forever, and I can't afford that.

However good you are at persuading a customer to buy more, be sure he knows what he has agreed to before it is too late. Otherwise you have made a bad sale. And not only have you hurt yourself by hurting your customer. You have also hurt me, because one bad reputation hurts us all. So don't foul up our nest with cheap tricks.

Remember that nobody—not even me—sells everybody. You don't have to twist anybody's arm or tell lies to make a good living in this selling business. All you have to do is use your head and plant enough seeds and fill enough seats. If you do it right, you'll be able to make a fine income and live with your conscience. I have proved that it can be done.

Closing: If he comes that far, he wants to buy. Never forget that and you'll win a lot.

18

Winning After the Close

The first thing I do after I make a sale is to prepare a file card on the buyer with everything I know about him and about what he bought. At the same time, a special thank-you letter goes out to the customer. I guess it's a pretty obvious thing to do—to thank the customer for buying from me. But you would be surprised how many salesmen don't do it. This means that my thank-you is noticed in that house, because it is so rare.

My thank-you tells the customer how happy I was to sell him (or her) the car that he (or she) wanted. It also reminds him that I will pay $25 for anybody he sends in to me who buys a new car. This is a very good time to remind him about being a birddog. You just told him when he got the car, and now you are reminding him when he is showing off the car and talking about it to neighbors and at the plant. I have a rule that I send out the thank-you on the very same day as the sale, so I never forget.

A lot of salesmen want to turn their back on a customer as

soon as they have made the delivery. If something is wrong with the car and the person brings it in, some salesmen even hide from the customer. They consider customer complaints and problems as annoyances that will finally go away. But that is the worst attitude you can have.

I look at it this way: Service problems and other customer complaints are a normal part of all business, regardless of what you sell. If you handle them properly, they can help you sell a lot more in the future. When a new car comes in with a bad problem for service, the service department people know they are supposed to notify me if I sold it. I will go out and try to pacify the customer. I'll tell him I will make sure that the work is done right, and that he will be happy with everything about the car. That is part of my job. And if the customer has still worse problems, my job is to take his side and make sure his car runs the way it should. I will fight for him with the mechanics, with the dealer, and with the factory.

If anybody buys a lemon from me—and it *can* happen—then I am going to turn the lemon into a peach. I will do whatever is necessary to get the car right. Sometimes I will even make an investment out of my own pocket. Most places, for instance, do not guarantee wheel alignment, even on a new car. After all, a fellow hits a pot hole or drives over a curb on the first day he has the car, and the alignment can go out. But if a customer comes back and asks for an alignment job, I will make sure he gets it and pay for it out of my own pocket. It costs me only about $6 tax-deductible, and it makes the customer feel I really want him to be happy. (But I also politely tell the customer that he cannot expect to get a second one free.)

The value of taking the customer's side is obvious. I become a friend, you come back to me for your next car, and you tell a lot of people about me if I stand behind you. That is one of the best ways to make customers into believers, believers in you and in your interest in their satisfaction.

I look at a customer as a long-term investment. I'm not just going to sell him that one car and then tell him to shove it when he is not satisfied with that car. I expect to sell him every car he is ever going to buy. And I want to sell his friends and his relatives. And, when the time comes, I want to sell his children their cars too. So when somebody buys from me, he is going to love that experience and he is going to remember it and remember me and talk about it to everybody he runs into who needs a car. I look at every customer as if he is going to be like an annuity to me for the rest of my life. So they have to be happy. They have to believe in me.

I think people buy from me because they are tired of getting hustled. They are tired of getting hurt. They know what has happened to them when a salesman hits them for a high price and then runs and hides when they need his help to get the car right. They know when that happens. They may have been gullible once. All you have to do is turn your back on a customer once, and he knows he has been hustled and conned and lied to.

But not my customers. When somebody comes in who is in a hurry because he needs a car bad, a lot of salesmen will be tempted to shove it to him good. They will take advantage of his need and hit him for a fat price, maybe $600 more than he would have to pay if he shopped a little. But he has no time to shop. When I run into a customer in that situation, I may not give the car away to him. Why should I? If he's willing to make a fast deal without shopping, I'll make a good profit for the dealer and for me. That's fair to everybody. But I am not going to hose a customer just because he happens to need something in a hurry. Look at it this way: A person who is in a hurry and is willing to pay more than he should is going to find out soon enough what was done to him. And then he is going to hit the ceiling and start bad-mouthing the car, the dealer, and the salesman. Who needs that? Not me, and I can probably afford a few losses. But you never know who is going to cost you a big annuity. And besides, I like it when my customers are happy. It makes me happy.

Make a Lemon into a Peach

When a customer drives into the service department with a genuine lemon, it can take me and my people a lot of time and energy making phone calls and finding the places to exert pressure to make that car right. Buying from me can be worth as much as $500 more than buying from another salesman, just because of the way I take care of customers who have problems. I don't make a customer pay more for that kind of quality service. He gets it no matter how good a deal he gets. I don't write down on his card that he bought cheap from me and that I don't have to do anything else for him. Everybody gets the same quality of service from me.

I think that should work in any field. If I buy a suit during a sale, I expect it to fit as well as if I bought at the top price. And if I get the feeling that they are trying to avoid doing enough alterations to make the suit fit, I'm going to lean on them to get it right. And I'm going to remember their treatment when I want another suit.

Automobile service is a big mystery to a lot of people. In the old days, cars were simple and every boy thought he knew all there was to know about how they worked and how to fix them. But these days cars are a lot more complicated than they used to be. Even though cars are better, a lot of people feel very helpless when things go wrong. I know a few people who have taken night-school courses in auto repairs, just so they'll know what the mechanic is talking about.

That gets us back to lemons. They can happen. They don't happen very often. But they do happen, maybe because an inspector at the factory had a hangover, maybe because a supplier goofed on an important subassembly. I don't mean to put down anybody in this industry. But sometimes a car comes off the line with a whole string of things wrong. It'll run well enough to drive off the assembly line and into the lot, and it will get past the final inspection. But then everything will hit the fan. I guess it's just a matter of the odds. One car can need adjustment to the transmission, another one has a piston that doesn't fit its cylinder, another one has a faulty gear in the rear axle. They can catch and fix that stuff pretty easily. But what happens when once in a couple of hundred thousand times it all happens to the same car? You get a lemon.

You come in with one thing wrong and it gets fixed. Then a few days later another thing goes sour, and you're back. In a lot of dealerships, their attitude is: Here comes that creep again. Well, let me tell you that when a guy gets a lemon, the only creeps are the people who won't do right by him.

It is not so easy to take care of lemons. I keep on very good terms with the people in the service department, buying them coffee in the mornings, gifts when their wives have babies, and things like that. But those are business expenses, because I mean business when one of my customers comes in with service problems. I also know the right people to call at the Chevrolet offices. And when nothing else works, I'll call somebody downtown to make sure my customer gets what he is entitled to.

All this costs me money and takes a good piece of time. But I don't think I have a choice. Just think about somebody lying there in a funeral home, and watch all the people coming in to pay their last respects. A man comes home, shaves, changes clothes, and maybe misses his bowling night to go see his friend for the last time. Think of the pulling power of that one guy lying in that satin-lined box. And there will be about 250 more people going through the same thing to see him. Everybody has that kind of pulling power, and none of us in the profession of selling can afford to jeopardize one single customer, because of those 250 people his life influences.

As you know, people talk a lot about cars. In many parts of the country it is the favorite topic of conversation between people, even more than the weather. And what I keep thinking is that somewhere out there, people are telling a story about how they bought a new car and everything started going wrong with it. They kept coming back for service but never got it fixed right, so they won't ever buy that kind of car again. And then one person starts telling the same story, only he ends up saying, "I told my salesman, Joe Girard, about my problems, and before I knew it, that car was running better than new." I know that people say things like that about the way I treat them, because I hear it. Whenever people come in and ask for me by name, I always ask them how they heard about me. It's a great opener. And you'd be surprised how many of them mention that somebody else told them what good deals and good treatment he got from me.

I don't mean to sound like some kind of tin god, but I think that does a lot for the whole profession. You can be sure that it does a lot for my business.

I hope that by this time you understand that I do a lot of things that other salesmen don't do. And I also hope you understand that what I do works for everybody. I am good to my customers. They know I really care about them and they believe in me. But I don't do anything for love. I do it for money. I have often said that the thing I like to do most in the world is sleep. It's my hobby and it's my favorite occupation, so when I have to get out of bed in the morning, somebody is going to pay for it.

But when I do treat my customers well, nobody goes out and says, "Girard doesn't really mean it. He only does it for the money." What I say is that I do really mean it, *and* I do it for the money. But it is a lot more pleasant to be nice to customers than to treat them like mooches and run and hide when they come in with troubles. And you make a lot more money by making your customers believers.

I know a man who used to buy all his clothes in one store from one salesman. He had walked into the store after seeing something in the window that he liked. The salesman who was up sold him and stayed with him. He would buy two or three suits a year from the man, and he didn't even need them, because he mostly didn't wear suits in his work. But the salesman took the trouble to find out what he liked and he would always do a number with the fitter when the man bought something. And sometimes he would tell him when he came in that he didn't think there was anything new that the customer would like. That was almost a challenge to the man to try to prove the salesman was wrong.

Anyway, one day he came in and asked for his salesman. Somebody came over and said that the man had retired, and then walked away. The customer hung around for a while looking at suits on the rack and even tried on one jacket. But nobody went over to him. He finally left and never came back again. So don't tell me that the relationship between the salesman and the customer isn't important.

I sell something that hundreds of thousands of other salesmen sell. A Chevrolet is a Chevrolet, you probably think. You can buy them in any town in the country. They're all alike. Right? Wrong! A Chevrolet sold by Joe Girard is not just a car. It is a whole relationship between me and that customer and his family and his friends and the people he works with. About 250 people.

You must be thinking that you have heard all this before. But I'll keep saying it, because I believe it and I know it works. It is the most obvious thing in the world to me, and it makes my business life very interesting and very profitable. But I will keep saying it, because even though it is obvious to me, it must not be very obvious to anybody else. Otherwise how come there are so many salesmen who barely make a living, and so many customers who think all salesmen are rich hustlers?

I've been telling you how important the after-sale phase is. I've told you how I always send a thank-you to every customer. I've given you some idea of how I take care of my customers when they have service problems with the cars I have sold them. So you get the idea that I stay with them as much as possible. Not only do I do the things I have described, but I also do one other thing.

Keep in Touch

Even if I never hear from the customer after the sale, I keep in touch. A lot of salesmen take their commissions and then forget about the customer, especially if there are no problems with the car. But, as you might expect, I look at things a lot differently. If I sell someone a car, they'll get my thank-you and they'll get my help with the service department if they need it. But even if they don't need help, they are going to hear from me.

A few weeks or months after I make the sale, I'll go through my file of recent customers and start calling them on the telephone. You would think that might be asking for trouble, but for me it is asking for future business and insuring that I get it. Just think about the typical experience of the average person buying a car from the average salesmen. When it is over, the customer is relieved just to have got out of there in one piece.

But with my customers it is different. I work hard, and they know it. When it is over, they are relieved too, but it is not because they escaped from the clutches of a high-pressure salesman, but because they got through an experience in which they started out full of fear and ended up feeling satisfied that they got better than they expected.

And then I pick up the phone, dial, and ask how the car is. I usually call during the daytime and get the wife. If I haven't seen them since they took delivery, then I figure they have had no problems. The wife usually will say that the car is fine. I'll ask if there's been any trouble. I'll remind her about coming in for the series of checkups necessary to keep the warranty in operation. And I'll tell her to be sure and tell her husband that if he has any problem at all with the car, any rattle, any mileage problem, or whatever, he should bring it in and ask for me. Then I'll ask if she knows of anybody who is looking to buy a car. I'll suggest friends and relatives and remind her that I will pay $25 for any customer who buys from me. If she says her brother-in-law was talking the other night about how beat-up his car is, I'll ask her for his name and number. And I'll also ask her to do me a favor and please call him, and I'll call him later. Then I remind her about the $25 and say goodbye.

Now chances are that this woman will tell her husband that I called and asked about them and whether the car was O.K. If he has never bought from me before, he might fall out of his chair, because everybody thinks that no salesman, especially a car salesman, ever gives a damn about the customer after the sale. And maybe I'll be able to sell her brother-in-law a car. So that extends the chain of goodwill and good business, because she gets that $25 birddog fee and her brother-in-law becomes the second satisfied customer in the family. And now I have two locked-in buyers every three or four or five years.

My Way Is Better

If what I am describing is so obvious, how come most salesmen never do it? I know that I am not smarter than average. And I know that I am not a nicer person. But perhaps I have just figured it out better, and put the whole selling process together. Maybe that's because I came to it late, didn't have the usual bad advice, and had to invent my own methods. I didn't know all the stuff that most salesmen know about hanging around and waiting for a mooch or a creep or a flake. And maybe, also, my need to succeed was greater. But one thing I know for sure is that there is something about that moment when salesmen finally get the order. It clouds their minds. They got what *they* wanted, and they forget all the smart things they should know about follow-up and keeping the customer happy for the next sale or referral.

I tell you this because I understand it. I understand this desire to make the sale and just hold the money in your hand. I understand it as well as anybody, maybe even better, because I understand the feeling well enough to keep it from defeating me. If I make $150 for an hour's work, I know the temptation to think that's how it goes. But when I feel that temptation coming on, I also feel the cure for it.

What's the cure? It is using your head. Nobody who sells cars makes $150 in an hour or even two. Either you have spent a lot of time and money building business, planting the seeds, filling the Ferris wheel seats—or you have spent a lot of hours doing nothing. If you sell one car a day and make $150, which is a pretty big average commission, you didn't make $150 for an hour's work. You made $150 for a day's work. Now that is not bad. In fact, if you sold a car a day, you would be well above average as a car salesman. But you would not be making $150 an hour.

I sell more than five cars every day, and I am the world's greatest salesman as far as the *Guinness Book of World Records* is concerned. And I know that I have to spend a lot of time and money to do it. It costs me a lot of my commissions to do the kind of business I do. But it is worth it, because I sell more, feel better about my work, and—even with what I spend to get business—still get to keep more after taxes than any other retail automobile salesman in this country. There is nothing about that in the Guinness book, but I'll bet it is true. So if you are listening to me, keep on listening, because this is all about satisfaction and money. And nobody can tell me that all the effort it takes to sell nearly 1,400 cars and make around $200,000 a year isn't worth it, if you are a real pro in our business.

Keep selling after the close—the money gets even bigger.

19

All the Help
You Can Get

I have been telling you all the things I do to build my business, to keep the customers coming in to ask for me and buy cars from me. And you have probably been sitting there taking it all in, but thinking that no single human being could do all that and still find time to eat a couple of times a day and get home to change clothes once a week.

Let's look at my history again. In my first full year of car selling, 1963, I sold 267 units. Anybody in the business will tell you that a salesman who sells 267 cars makes a good living. No award winner. No mention in Guinness. But a pretty good buck, then or now. My output went up to 307 the next year, and to 343 in 1965. By 1966 I had begun to take a good look at what was working for me, and I began focusing on those things that I could see were producing the most results for me. In other words, I had learned where my strengths were, and I started using them as best I could. I was sending out my own direct mail. I was beginning to promote birddogs.

And I had learned by then that my customers weren't mooches.

So how did I do in the first year that I really was operating out of experience and careful self-analysis? How did I make out in the first year that I was no longer operating on instinct and feel? In 1965 I sold 343 cars and trucks, but in 1966 my total soared to 614 units. I was selling a lot of cars and trucks, and I was making a lot of money. But I was beating my brains out, staying late at the office to catch up on paper work and telephone calls. At the end of the year 1969, the man who does my income taxes looked at my figures and said, "Joe, you're knocking yourself out and you're paying half of it to the government. Why don't you spend some money to get some help, and hire some arms and legs to help you? It'll only cost you 50¢ of every dollar you spend. Besides, you'll be able to concentrate more on the things you do and like best [*closing the sale*], and you'll be able to pay somebody else to do the routine stuff."

Now just read over what he said to me. I'm indebted to my accountant for possibly saving my life and ultimately making me more sales and more money. I can't put it any better than that to any of you who have reached a fairly high tax bracket. In fact, I have talked to my accountant about it lately, and he says that salespeople who make more than $20,000 a year working alone can afford to pay for at least some part-time outside help. The key point is that I end up with a lot more money for every dollar I spend on outside help. It is like a capital investment. Instead of buying a machine, I buy the time of a human being to free me to do what I do best, which is "closing."

Remember that nobody sells all alone. To sell your customers, you use help whether you think of it that way or not. You use the telephone, you use the mail service, and you make use of other people in your organization such as secretaries, filing clerks, mechanics, tailors, and others. You have other people to do what they can do better than you can.

I started using outside help when my mailing list started taking too much of my time. I hired high school students part-time to stuff and address my mailings. You may never have more than a handful of names on your mailing list. But if the list ever gets to more than a few hundred and the number of mailings gets up there, you can't possibly afford the time it takes to do the routine stuff, unless you think you can't make more than $1.50 or $2.00 an hour when you are working. I'm serious. That's the way to look at the numbers. If you can only make $5.00 an hour (and I'm sure you can do a lot better than that), you are still way ahead paying somebody $1.50 to do some of the nonselling chores. Because even if you get only $5.00, you are $3.50 ahead by hiring somebody else to free you. That is simple mathematics, and there is no way to argue it away, unless you *like* to do nonselling work. And if that's the case, you ought to get out of the business. You would be happier not selling.

After I had that talk with my tax man, I hired a young man I had met a few weeks earlier. A friend of mine had sent him to see me to learn about the selling business. I called him in and put him to work greeting customers for me. By that time, a lot of people were coming in and asking for Joe Girard. Often there would be people waiting while I was closing another customer. I lost some of them because they got tired of waiting and left, or let another salesman in the showroom handle them. Besides that, I was losing customers whom I was about to close, because I would be interrupted by other people coming in or calling me. I never take phone calls now when I am closing a customer. I have somebody to handle my business calls. And I don't get personal calls, because I tell everybody not to call me at work unless there is a genuine emergency.

So I hired this fellow to help me. I trained him to greet people and explain to them that I was tied up at the moment, but that he would help them as much as he could. He would interview and qualify them, show them around a car, and answer their questions. Also he would take a careful look at their trade-in, and take them for a demonstration ride. Afterward, he would call me in my closing office and tell me what he found out. I trained him to look for clues to hobbies, travels, family needs, and evidence that the prospect had shopped other dealers. He would also tell me the condition of the car the customer drove in.

My income increased by more than what it cost me to employ this assistant. He made money and I made money. Once I had seen the value of this employee, I knew that it was the way to go. In 1966 I sold almost twice as many cars without help as I had sold the year before, but it practically killed me. I could not possibly have gone through another year like that without help. But I couldn't stand still. I had to keep breaking records. And after I had broken everybody else's records, I had to go on breaking my own.

My Biggest Competitor

You want to know whom I compete with? I compete with Joe Girard. What I did today I want to beat tomorrow. There is nobody else to compete with, because I have passed them all. I read an article somewhere about a fellow in Illinois who is supposed to be the biggest Cadillac salesman. And I guess he is, but I looked at his figures, and I realized that even though Cadillac sells for twice as much as Chevrolet, I not only outsell him 3 to 1 on units but I probably sell twice as many dollars' worth as he does. And I know that my commission take is more than twice his. So who else is there to compete with except Joe Girard? Nobody!

The only way I can keep beating my own record is to spend some of my money to hire people to help me increase my output. Otherwise I would reach a limit where I would never be able to grow any more. And that would kill me. It would also hold down my volume and income. And selling is my joy, and money is my reward.

But what is most important from a business standpoint is that you get the greatest possible leverage by hiring people to help free you to do your most productive work. And if you are a professional salesman, your greatest skill and your greatest joy is closing. That is the kill, that is the victory, the power and the glory of selling.

I use my help now to allow me to focus most of my working time on closing. Back in 1970 I hired my first full-time employee, a young man named Nick Renz. He is still with me, and he is now my right hand, running the administrative part of the operation and helping me with other business ventures, especially my speaking work with sales groups and my sales film program. My son Joey also works full time for me. Each earns a salary that a lot of salesmen would consider good. By paying them good money, I make even more than I ever could operating alone.

The truth is, as I have pointed out, that none of us operates as one man. We don't make what we sell. A lot of salesmen don't deliver. We all operate as part of a huge economic system where everybody depends on everybody else. The trick is to be in command of at least a part of that system, so that you make a profit from other people's efforts, even though you pay them a fair price for their work.

My son Joe is now in charge of the whole front end of our operation. By this I mean that he greets our customers, lines them up as they await their turn, and gets all the information he can from them. He is a lot more than a greeter. He is our intelligence agent. He shows them the car, presents its features, gives them a demonstration ride, and handles the trade-in. He is on the lookout for all the clues that I mentioned earlier. He does most of the job of trying to find out what kind of person we are dealing with, what his interests are, what he wants to buy, what he is afraid of, and what we can do to sell him.

Shortly after Joe passes the customer in to my closing office, he calls me from the showroom on the phone. I say all kinds of things into the phone, pretending I am talking to somebody else. But what is really happening is that Joe is giving me his report on the customer. He'll tell me the mileage on the car, the condition of the tires, plus all kinds of things like a Disneyland bumper sticker, an empty box of shotgun shells, or anything else that will give me ammunition to use in disarming the customer and getting him over his fear of buying what he came in to buy.

I have said a lot about that fear. But just try to think of what that person is going through. He is probably an average working-class guy, and he has to spend maybe $5,000 on an automobile. That is as much as he may make in four months, and he has a hard time forgetting this basic fact. What we are trying to do is to get his thinking to the point where he will make that purchase. Now you have to bear in mind that nobody forced him into our place of business. However much mail, however much persuasion from birddogs, he is not going to come in until he wants a car and needs a car. What we are trying to do is make his decision come true in the most painless way possible. And the more information about the customer that Joe passes to me in that phone call, the quicker and more effectively I can close this customer and go on to the next one. When I say more effectively, I mean putting him into the best possible car he needs to go to work, to take his family places, and to get to his spare-time activities—at a price he can afford. Remember that I never want to deceive a man about the amount of his monthly payments or the number he will have to make. I want him to be able to manage every aspect of that car, including paying for it. Because if it hurts him to pay for it, I may still earn a commission, but he is not going to like his memory of buying from me. I guess you could say that, by using help, I can do a better job of getting the right car at the right price for the right person, because my intelligence operation works better.

Joe also helps me to keep our customers sold, because it is

his job to take their deposit checks to the bank to get them "hammered"—that's our slang word for certified. Once I have the customer's deposit and his signature on the order form and, I hope, his body in a car, Nick takes over and handles all the after-sale administrative work. He works out the details of the credit, insurance, and registration arrangements, sends out the thank-you, does all the paper work for the office, and makes sure that all the proper information on the customer goes into our files.

What do I do? I close. I get the customers to the point where they say yes and mean yes, not "maybe" or "I'll let you know."

A Great Performance Is the Truth

I have said that selling is acting. I put on a performance for my customers. I don't lie any more than an actor or a comedian on a stage is lying. I play the part of a friend, an adviser, a persuader. When you see Carroll O'Connor playing Archie Bunker, you know he is not Archie Bunker, and there is no Archie Bunker. But you also believe that Carroll O'Connor *is* Archie Bunker. He is not telling you a lie when he gives a great performance. And neither am I. I am all the things I pretend to be, and I am also Joe Girard looking to get a thrill from selling another car, and looking to make some more money.

I need help to get the script ready and to help me get the audience out of the theater after the performance. I used to do the whole job myself, and I did it pretty well. I won a few awards even before I started employing other people to help me. But now, with their help, I am doing even better. And the more you make, the more you can afford to use help so that you earn even more. Once you are working every minute of every day, there is no other way to grow except by using other people intelligently and efficiently. No other way.

That's not completely true. A lot of people ask me how come I never went into business for myself and became a dealer. The simple answer is that I am a salesman. It's true that I did a lot of other things in the first 35 years of my life before I became a salesman. But for the most part I didn't do them very well. It wasn't until I discovered selling—needed to discover it—that I really found something I loved and never wanted to stop doing. But now selling is the great joy, the great satisfaction, and the great money producer of my life.

I could probably raise the money to become a dealer. And I could probably run a pretty good operation. But I don't want to. I am having too good a time selling. I have two top people who earn good money handling my operations. I don't have to watch them. I have no personnel, capital, security, or management decisions to make. My dealer makes more money than I do, but he is entitled to it because he has a lot of money invested in his business, and because he has a lot more business responsibilities than I do. But I make a lot more money net than many other dealers.

The Biggest Thrill of My Life

The worst thing about being a dealer is that I would not have any time to sell. I would probably make more money, but not that much more. And I would have to give up the biggest thrill of my life, the excitement of closing five or more sales almost every day. No dealer can ever expect to do that. And I wouldn't give it up for anything. Not that owning a dealership isn't a perfectly respectable way to make a living. It surely is. But it just isn't as much fun. I get it both ways— the fun and the money. I don't think there is any other way to match the joy of selling.

About the only other things that excite me as much are the other activities I have gotten into in recent years that relate to selling. As I have said, I give talks to salesmen and I perform in and produce sales training films. In a real way, they are like selling belly to belly. In some ways they are even better, because they are more of the same.

I have talked about leverage, and about the thrill of selling a car. But I have found that these two other activities let me put leverage and the thrill of selling together in a very special way. It is not exactly what this book is about, but let me explain it to you, and I think you'll understand that it is quite closely connected to what we are talking about. When I stand on a platform and talk to other salesmen, there are a couple of payoffs. One is like the feeling I get when I finally close a customer in my office. On a platform I get the same feeling, only more of it, because I know that I am getting across to a roomful of people. Afterward, they come up and tell me how much of what I say has affected them. They tell me and they write me that nobody else ever tells them as much about how selling really is because nobody else who gives sales talks has had as much on-the-job experience as I have. That's part of the excitement of making films, too, knowing that the people who watch them have never seen anything as true to life about their business. I'm proud of what I do and of how well I do it, and I get a thrill out of knowing that I am changing the professional lives of other salesmen.

I like selling and helping other salesmen a lot more than I like the idea of running a dealership. That's why I have started the Joe Girard Sales Course. Over the years I have seen many people try their hand at selling only eventually to give it up or settle for an average income. I have always believed that if these people could have had the proper guidance and training they would probably be living today in a manner which they never would have thought possible.

But just remember that when you are alone with a customer, face to face, in that crucial confrontation, there are a lot of other people and services working for you. And you should look for and get all the help you can afford. That may mean birddogs, as well as part-time and full-time help. Because leverage—extending yourself most efficiently—is the way to make the most of your time and your skills.

Anybody who wants to, really wants to, can build the kind of operation I have. I built the whole thing gradually, and paid for it out of part of the extra money my growth was bringing in. More help, more customers, more money, more help, more customers, more money, and on and on and on. That's the way it happened for me, and that's the way it can happen for you.

Don't think that I am loafing because I went from some part-timers to one and then two other people full time. I am working just as long hours as I used to, but I keep on doing better, because what I am doing all the time now is what I do best—closing. A surgeon doesn't clean his own instruments. He hires lower-priced people for that so that he can concentrate on where the big money is—the surgery. And that's what we are, surgeons, and we too should concentrate all our time on the surgery. Let somebody else prepare the patient, do the tests, get the history, so we can do the cutting through of the customer's fears and get to the inside, where we can find and cut away the sales resistance.

Get all the help you can—it builds gross and net.

20

Spending and Getting

There are a lot of ways to put together what I have been saying about myself and our profession. One way is to understand that all of the most effective ways to bring in customers and sell them cost money. You have to buy business if you want to eliminate the risks and be assured of a steady and growing income. That is the same situation that any other businessman is in. In fact, that's what any business is about: deciding what are the best ways to spend money to get the most money back. With us it is a matter of spending time as well as money. But since we know what is the most important and most valuable thing we do, all we have to worry about is being smart in *how* we buy business.

It doesn't take much to understand the value of birddogs because you have to pay only when you have got what you paid for: the sold customer. So it makes sense to spend time and money to get more birddogs. There is no problem in understanding that direct mail that gets read is worth the cost, and direct mail that doesn't get read isn't worth sending even if it is free.

I am sure I have convinced you that my birddog recruiting and my direct mail are worth the investment. But you may think that they are worth it only to me and that it wouldn't pay for you to try something similar. But what I am trying to say is that I knew in advance, before I spent the money and started the sales rolling in, that those things would work. That's why I did them in the first place. I was able to start them on a small scale and build. And that is how you can do it too.

But you have to be able to look at the situation in your business and find out what are your best opportunities. For instance, the wife of a service writeup man goes to the hospital for an operation. He is good at his job and helps me a lot with my customers' service problems. I want to send a gift. Everybody sends flowers and candy to sick people. But then the stuff gets thrown out. And the longer it lasts, the more times they will think of Joe Girard. So I figure what would be a good lasting gift, and I send a plant instead of flowers. The plant stays in the house and people always remember who sent it. Now I have an arrangement with a florist for sending gifts whenever I think they are needed. I send a terrarium, which is for plants, but it is also like a piece of furniture. People don't throw such a gift away. It is special, so it is worth more than what it cost me. And that's the game— whatever you do should be worth more than what it costs you. That doesn't mean it has to be cheap. Instead, think of how much good it can do for your business-building. Think of how much it will do to get people to think of you as a nice guy and talk about you to their friends and relatives. That is the kind of business judgment you need to make sure that you are putting your time and your money to work most efficiently. This is what the people at the Pentagon call "cost-effective." It doesn't mean cheap; it does mean getting your money's worth, however much or little you decide to spend.

The Spending That More Than Pays Its Way

Gifts, terrariums, you're thinking, that's for the high rollers. Not true. They are for everybody. Just stop and think of what happens when you hear that a customer is sick and you send a get-well card. What salesman does that? So here comes this card to the guy in the hospital. He's got nothing to do but watch television and wait for visitors. You send just a card —never mind plants—and you know that this customer is going to remember you and talk about you to everybody who comes in: "I got a get-well card from Joe Girard, the fellow who sells Chevvies." Or you are a clothing salesman, and you send something to the fellow who runs the tailor shop when he is out sick. Now a customer comes in who wants to buy three suits, but he's going on a trip and needs them tomorrow. If there is any way of getting those alterations done by tomorrow, you know that your friend in the tailor shop will find it for you.

The more money you spend wisely, the more people you can put to work, talking you up, helping you sell, buying.

I have said a lot about making judgments and spending money. But there are also important ways to invest time. And one of the most important is thinking smart. Whatever your business is about, however it works, it can be improved. There is no perfect way to do business. You can always find some way to do things better if you spend enough time thinking about it. But you have to think in ways that will help you get new ideas. You have to look at the most tried-and-true methods as if you could rearrange them and make them work better for you.

Here's a classic example: A young man comes out of a life insurance company training program and starts looking for business. Everybody in the program has been told that one of the ways is to use a directory of business executives. So this young man does what he is told and gets hold of a copy of the directory. He sits down, opens the first page, and stops. He thinks to himself that 20 other guys who were in the training program are doing the same thing. They are all sitting down with the directory and opening it to the first page. This means everybody will go after the same prospects to sell them the same thing. *Why should I bother?* the man asks himself. *But what can I do to get ahead of them?* Then he hits on a very simple, obvious idea that nobody else had suggested. Instead of opening the book to "A," he opens it near the middle, at "N." As a result, he calls prospects who hardly ever get called, he gets a lot of appointments, and he sells lots of insurance policies right from the start.

That man is a very prosperous insurance agent now, and he believes that stopping to think of a better way to operate was the thing that contributed most of all to his success. After that, he says, there was nothing to it. I don't believe him completely, and neither does he, because we both know that he works very smart all the time. He is always looking for new and different ways to approach the same old problems. And by looking, he probably finds them more often than other salesmen.

Don't Be Afraid to Do It Differently—It's Usually Better

You could say the same thing about my direct mail program, about my gifts, and about the whole way that I do business. It is a lot different from the way other people used to sell cars, and different from the way most other people still do. I was ignorant of all the "wisdom" of the business when I started, so I developed my own methods. Not all at once, but gradually, as I kept looking for better ways to build my business and sell more. I am not trying to say that I invented everything that I do. I borrowed a lot of my ideas from other people and other businesses. Does everybody in your business work a list from the beginning of the alphabet? Then why not steal one from the insurance man and start in the middle, or maybe you should try the end. But whatever you come up with, the important thing is not to be put off by the guys who tell you that you can't do it because it has never been done before.

This may be the stupidest attitude in the world: that something can't be done because it hasn't been done before. If that was true, there would never be anything new in the world. None of the inventions, none of the great new ideas, would exist. And the same is true for your business. Who says something won't work because it hasn't been done before? Just the people who don't want competition. But that is what our profession is about—competition. Everybody who sells is competing all the time against other people selling the same thing or other things. A customer can't decide whether to wait six months instead of buying from me today, because he also wants to spend the money on a boat or a vacation. So a boat dealer and a travel agent are selling against me, besides the thousands of other people selling Chevrolet and every other car in the world.

The biggest advantage you can get is to come up with a better way of reaching and selling your customers. Good ideas are always worth the time it takes to think of them. And they are always worth the money they may cost to put into operation. "R & D," they call it, research and development. You should have it too. You should always be looking at new things to try and new ways to test the value of what you are already doing. That way you will be constantly looking to improve the most important product that you sell—which is you.

The trick is always to look for new ways to do old things. The unexpected can be the most effective. I have mentioned before that I am very sensitive to ethnic slurs. A guy would start in about "dagos" and "wops," and I would start boiling. Whether I hit him or not, I would get mad and lose the sale. Finally, one day I decided that my business during working hours was selling cars to anybody who wanted one. I didn't want to lose business or teeth getting into fights about my being Sicilian. So I did a simple thing. I called the printer and told him to print me a new batch of business cards. Instead of putting my legal name, Girardi, on them, I told him to drop the *i* at the end and make it just plain Girard. I didn't change my name legally. I just decided to take on a stage name, like John Wayne and Dean Martin and thousands of other people. Even that Cadillac salesman I mentioned before drops the last part of his name in business, because it is too long to write and to pronounce.

That was a simple idea, but it took me a long time to figure it out. Yet once I decided to do it, it changed my life, because it eliminated one of the most important problems in my business life without changing anything in my private life. I have received hate mail from other Italians who think I changed my name legally because I was ashamed of what I am. But that's not true. I did it for the same reason that I don't wear fancy suits to work and for the same reason that I do many other things in my business. I did it because I wanted my customers to look at me as the person they believe in and want to buy a car from. I don't care what they think about the real world. I want them to come to my show and trust me and believe in me and buy from me. So I make sure that I give a good performance by wearing the right clothes, giving them a comfortable environment to be in with me, and carrying a name they will remember only because they like to buy from me. If they have prejudices, that's their problem. I don't want to know about it. In the world where I am selling them, I want nothing to interfere with their trust in Joe Girard.

I am not recommending that anybody change his name. But what I am trying to say is that you should look at everything, including your name, to see if you can improve your selling efficiency. Changing my business name worked for me. Something else can work for you, whether you think it up yourself or steal it from some other business. Looking around for ideas, research and development is something that is always worth the investment of your time and money. But when I say time and money, I should also mention a third ingredient—patience.

Patience is not an easy thing when you don't have unlimited time or money. But without it you may never get the fat payoff that you have started in motion. When I started recruiting birddogs, I knew that it would take time before I would start seeing new business come in. But I just kept on looking and recruiting. And I kept after the people after I signed them up. They got mail reminders from me about the $25, and a lot of them also got phone calls. You plant the seeds and you have to water them, and then you have to do other things while you are waiting for them to sprout. But they will sprout if you have executed the first steps properly. You can bet on that, because if you made the effort and have the patience, you have stacked the deck in your favor, and you can't lose in the long run.

But patience alone, just standing by the door, will not tilt the odds your way. You have to make your own odds by spending time and money to develop your own methods to bring in the customers and the money.

Time and money well invested will build your business tremendously. Always look for new and better ways to do it.

21

There Is No
Last Chapter

If you have come this far with me, I hope you are not still
looking for magic words or formulas or phrases to say to yourself in the mirror. Life doesn't work that way, and business
doesn't either. There are no secrets; there is no magic. The
process of successful selling means endless use of your mental
resources. There is no final chapter. The process just keeps on
starting over and over.

It took me 35 years of drifting to get to the beginning of the
process. But it took me only a few years from there to get to
the top. And I am at the top.

A lot of people out there, maybe millions, have heard of me.
And thousands have bought from me. They think they know
a lot about me, because I know a lot about them. They think
I have been to Yellowstone National Park. They think
that I have fished for salmon near Traverse City, Michigan.
They think I have an aunt who lives near Selfridge Air Force
Base. They think those things because they have been to Yel-

lowstone National Park and fish for salmon and live near Selfridge Field, and because I know about their lives.

They think they know my name and what I am like. They
have heard a lot about me. But the only thing they really care
about is what they get for their money when they buy from
me. They believe in me and in my deals, because they know
for sure that I give the best deals. And they are right about
that, which is all that really matters to them and to me.

Anybody Can Do What I Have Done

If there is anything like a secret in all that I have said, it is
the fact that anybody can do what I have done. You don't have
to be a genius. I never even finished high school. But I still
trust my eyes and ears and my feeling about how I like to be
treated, and I know what makes me buy from one person and
not from another one.

I have trained myself to remember at all times that everybody I meet can become important to my business life. I never
think of any person as just one sale. Never. I always think
about Girard's Law of 250; all the friends, relatives, fellow
bowlers, and co-workers who can turn out to be part of that
250. It doesn't take a computer expert to understand how this
law works. I know that the same 250 people who could bad-
mouth me for being lousy can be my customers. I never forget
that, and I don't believe that anybody else who sells can afford
to forget it.

You can be sure that if I am thinking about that many people all the time, I treat everybody very carefully, even people
with the worst possible credit ratings. After all, I was broke
plenty of times in my life. But I came back, and I have a top
credit rating now. So I figure that if somebody has had trouble
paying his bills, he can still be all right. And if you figure out
a way to finance him when his rating is low, you will make him
a believer for life.

That is why I am very careful even when a person has to have a co-signer to get his car loan. When I run into a case like that, I tell him to bring in his best buddy to help me verify his credit application, and to let me handle it. When a person hears that you want him to sign for a friend's loan, he usually starts talking about how he has a rule about never co-signing. But I try to avoid putting it all out front. I ask the man to look at the facts on the application and "just O.K. this for me." And I push the pen where he has to pick it up. If the man resists, I appeal to him on the basis of his friendship with my customer, reminding him how they fished together and went to high school together and chased girls together. I remind him of how they are best friends, and that his friend needs his help. And my customer reassures his friend that he will have no trouble making the payments, because his troubles are past and he has a good job. I have made it into a favor that the man can't refuse without losing his friend and looking bad in front of me. And he signs it.

I can do this because I really believe that people can change their lives, because I changed my life. Just so, you can change your life. When I get a co-signer's name on the form, I am expressing my belief that other people can come back from the bottom just like I did.

I never forget the night I spent in juvenile detention and the nights I slept in freight cars in the railroad yard. Now I sleep in a beautiful home in Grosse Pointe Shores, just a few blocks from where members of the Henry Ford II family live. As a present for my wife, I had a spectacular bathroom built with a marble tub and a sauna and columns all around the room. That alone cost me $32,000. That's more money than I ever made in any two years before I got into the selling profession.

If this sounds like I am bragging, I guess that I am, a little bit. But you didn't read this book to find out how good I am. You wanted to know how I became successful, and how you can too.

The message is that you can do it, because if I did it, starting when and where I did, then practically anybody can do it. But you have to *want* to do it. I know a lot of salesmen who are just as smart as I am, maybe smarter. And plenty of them are just as good closers, maybe even better, but they don't put it all together like I do, and like you can. They may be lazy, they may be content with just a little bit of the pie. But if you expect to get more, you have to want more. You have to know what you want so bad you can practically taste it. You have to motivate yourself the way I did when my wife told me there was no money for food for the kids. Maybe what you want that bad is to afford a separate place for your mother-in-law to live. Maybe you want a cabin cruiser. Maybe you want to take a trip to Paris. Then want it bad enough to make it affect your professional life. Look at everybody you meet as if he can give you what you want if you can get him to buy from you. And look into yourself to see why you like some people and don't like others, which is why you buy from some and not from others.

Think about the fear you have sometimes felt when you went to buy something. Then you can begin to understand what is going on in your customer's head when you meet him. Think of how people look for a friend when they are scared, and then be that friend. Make yourself a friend that your customer can trust and believe in.

It's a game, I have said. It's an act. But it is also real. If you are doing your job, you really do become that customer's friend. I don't mean that you bowl with him or invite him into your house. Not that kind of friend. But the kind that a person can trust to treat him fairly and decently. He comes in scared. He knows you are not interested in his health and welfare, but in your own. He knows you don't care about his wife and kids and what happened at the job today. But all of a sudden, he finds that you do care, because you are asking him about these things. Pretty soon he isn't as afraid any more. He starts to believe that maybe you do care about him. You let him talk and you listen. Before long, he trusts you enough to do what you say, which is to sign the order and buy from you.

The Most Valuable Asset in Selling

Now comes the test. He buys from you, but will he regret it? Not if he trusts you and believes in you. He won't regret it if he finds that you really did treat him fairly, and that you really did make sure he understood exactly what he was buying and for how much. After he leaves with his purchase is the time of the real test. He got out of there safe. Now he is living with his purchase, with what he trusted you enough to buy without being absolutely sure, beyond a reasonable doubt, that this was what he wanted to do. Now he is living with what you did to him and for him. And if you played the game fair and won the battle for both of you, you have created the most valuable asset in the selling business, a customer who trusts you because you helped him get what he needed and wanted.

That all sounds pretty simple. Nothing to it. Nothing, except getting your own head right. I have said over and over that you have to want and you have to know what you want. But that can make you greedy instead of a good salesman. That can push you into pushing the customer too hard. And whether you sell him or not, if you push too hard, you lose the customer. Even if he doesn't talk you down to his friends, he won't come back to you next time. You have to learn to control the wanting so that it makes you smart, not stupidly greedy.

You may start out every morning hating somebody: your boss, your mother-in-law, your dog, or your dead father. But you better find that out before you go to work. Because you can use these feelings to drive you toward good habits, not bad ones. Instead of trying to con and outsmart your customer, you can convert these feelings into wanting to win the customer over to your side.

I have never stopped trying to prove to my father that I was worth something. For too many years, I let his words destroy my motivation, because I was trying to make him like me by proving that he was right. I really did feel that if I did lousy and was a bum, he would like me because this would prove that he was right. But then I had to grow up. There was no way to survive if I kept believing I was no good. Now I play it the other way. I remember his saying that I was no good and use this memory to prove that he was wrong. Every time I make a friend out of a customer, I prove that he was wrong. I win my fight with him every time I sell a car, every time somebody believes in me and trusts me.

Instead of making me dumb and no good, his words and the memory of his fists and his strap make me smart, make me effective, make me an even better professional than I was before. Everybody who makes himself into something better has to fight the forces in him that want to be something worse. Everybody has those feelings in him. Both kinds, destructive and constructive. Winning is constructive. And if I could turn from a loser to a winner, and you know that I did it, then anybody can.

I didn't wake up one morning and go through a miraculous change. I didn't suddenly know how to treat customers, who to listen to, who to stay away from, how to get people to read my mail, how to get people to buy from me and like it.

It Can Happen to You

I have tried to explain to you how it happened to me. I have tried to do it in a way that will convince you that it can happen to you, if you make it happen. What I am talking about is not mental health or peace of mind. I am talking about selling. I am talking about all the time that you are working and thinking about work. That is a lot of the time in the life of any professional salesman. And it requires him to look at himself and what he wants and focus on how to get it. You have to do it every day. You have to remind yourself of what you want. And you have to think about how you get what you want and how you can get more of it.

That means you have to look at your work as a profession with right moves and wrong ones, with ideas and methods that work and others that don't work. You have to study yourself and your work so that you know what makes you effective. I have told you a lot about how I think and feel and work. I have told you a lot of details about my methods. I know that there is a lot there that you can use, because many salesmen have told me that they have learned from what I tell them. They have told me that what I do works for them. But the best of them go on to develop their own methods and techniques. They take off from mine and develop better variations. Or they may even come up with their own systems that work better than mine do—for them. And I know salesmen in completely different fields who have used my techniques and variations successfully even though they had never been used before in that business. We have all seen a group of new small retail businesses develop—boutiques, they call them, small stores, usually selling clothing, that offer very personal service. This means that even though you can buy everything you want by pushing a cart through a self-service store, people want personal service. They prefer to buy from people who act like they care about them: people who call them when something comes in that they want, who remember their birthdays and their interests, who write to them personally.

Anybody can run a boutique type of selling operation, no matter what you sell. Because what counts is not what kind of store you work in or what kind of merchandise you sell; what counts is how you treat your customers. That's the oldest, tiredest advice in the world, but it is also the truest. In a world of computers and self-service, a salesman who says *"thank you"* can look like a hero and a friend. You have to say it because you mean it. But why shouldn't you mean it? Somebody came in and bought from you and gave you money so you can feed your kids or go to Europe or buy a speedboat. You better mean it. You better believe that anybody who gives you money is not a mooch but a human being.

There is no last word to this book. The story doesn't end. It just keeps beginning again. But each time that it begins, each time you plant seeds or fill the seats, it should be a little more professional, a little more effective. The customers and the money grow gradually, but they grow. And the more you sell, the more fun and the more profit you have.

At the beginning, I said that if you read and listened and learned the way I learned and did what I did, you would be a better seller of whatever you sell and you would like your work and yourself better.

That guarantee still holds. If I did it, you can do it. I guarantee it.